D0186321

BRIGHT NEW IDEAS

10-Minute Games

AGES 5-11

Alison Milford

Evesham & Malvern Hills College
Library

33925

Author
Alison Milford

Editor
Wendy Tse

Assistant Editor
Aileen Lalor

Project Editor
Wendy Tse

Series designer
Joy Monkhouse

Designer
Erik Ivens

Illustrations
Garry Davies

Cover photographs
© Stockbyte

Published by Scholastic Ltd,
Villiers House,
Clarendon Avenue,
Leamington Spa,
Warwickshire
CV32 5PR

Printed by Bell & Bain Ltd, Glasgow

Text © Alison Milford 2005

5 6 7 8 9 0   7 8 9 0 1 2 3 4

Visit our website at www.scholastic.co.uk

British Library Cataloguing-in-Publication Data
A catalogue record for this book is available from
the British Library.

ISBN 0-439-97175-6
ISBN 978-0439-97175-1

Acknowledgements
The British Nutrition Foundation in conjunction
with The British Heart Foundation for the use of 'The
balance of good health game' adapted from text
used by both organisations which appeared in The
British Heart Foundation's booklet *Archie Beat's Picnic*
by Alison Milford.
Matt Buchanan for adaptations of the games 'No
you can't take me' and 'Gibberish sentences' from
the website www.childdrama.com © Matt Buchanan.
Steven Chase for the use of 'Geometry Bingo' from
www.aplusmath.com © 1998, Steven Chase (1998,
www.aplusmath.com).
Gary Clifford for the use of the map 'Isolated
farms' by Gary Clifford from *Primary Foundations:
Geography 7–9* by John Corn © 2000, Gary Clifford
(2000, Scholastic Limited).
The Scout Association for permitting adaptation
of the games 'Hit the Skittle' from *Indoor Games
for Scouts* edited by Rex Hazelwood © 1951, The
Boy Scouts Association; 'Through the legs', 'Who
is faster?', 'Telegrams', 'Move the football' 'Throw
it and Run' and 'Post Office Race' from *Scout
Games* compiled by Nigel Frankland © 1972, The
Boy Scouts Association; 'Material Relay' from *It's
Troop Night Again* by Delta and Theta © 1954,
The Boy Scouts Association (1954, The Boy Scouts
Association) Licence No. 0204.

Material from the National Curriculum © The
Queen's Printer and Controller of HMSO.
Reproduced under the terms of HMSO Guidance
Note 8
Material from the NNS and NLS © Crown Copyright.
Reproduced under the terms of HMSO Guidance
note 8

Every effort has been made to trace copyright
holders for the works reproduced in this book,
and the publishers apologise for any inadvertent
omissions.

The right of Alison Milford to be identified as the Author of this work has been asserted by her in accordance with the
Copyright, Designs and Patents Act 1988.

All rights reserved. This book is sold subject to the condition that it shall not, by way of trade or otherwise, be lent,
hired out or otherwise circulated without the publisher's prior consent in any form of binding or cover other than that
in which it is published and without a similar condition, including this condition, being imposed upon the subsequent
purchaser.

No part of this publication may be reproduced, stored in a retrieval system, or transmitted, in any form or by any
means, electronic, mechanical, photocopying, recording or otherwise, without the prior permission of the publisher.
This book remains copyright, although permission is granted to copy those pages marked 'photocopiable' for
classroom distribution and use only in the school which has purchased the book or by the teacher who has purchased
the book and in accordance with the CLA licensing agreement. Photocopying permission is given for purchasers only
and not for borrowers of books from any lending service.

Contents

EVESHAM COLLEGE
372.21
LIBRARY
33925

Chapter 5 – Art, design & technology

Chapter 6 – Music

Chapter 7 – Physical education

Chapter 8 – PSHE & citizenship

Introduction

Learning through games has increasingly become a valuable part of children's education. The fun and enjoyment of playing and mastering a game can motivate and enhance children's learning right across the curriculum. Children tend to absorb information much more effectively if they are having fun while doing it. Despite this, finding time to organise and play games can be quite difficult. One effective way is to have a resource of fun and accessible game ideas, such as those found in *10-Minute Games*, that can easily be incorporated into a busy timetable.

Using the book
The 10-minute games in this book can be used in many different ways, for example:
- to start off a lesson involving a particular skill or subject. This enables the children to focus their minds for the main part of the lesson.
- to conclude a lesson by allowing the children to consolidate the skills they have learned during the main part of the lesson.
- as a form of assessment.
- to revisit concepts and skills learnt in past lessons.
- as a fun and educational way to fill an unplanned extra 10 minutes.
- as a way to form relationships within the class.

The purpose of this book is to offer a range of fun and practical 10-minute games, covering the curriculum across the primary age range. The aim is for teachers, supply teachers, student teachers and teaching assistants to be able to dip into the book and find a 10-minute game for their future or immediate needs.

Each chapter looks at a different area of the curriculum. Games are often a popular method of teaching skills for different subjects such as physical education, literacy, science, maths, music and PHSE and so in this book you will find chapters dedicated to each area. There are also games which fit into the areas of history, geography, art, and design and technology. To make the games more accessible, some of them concentrate on generic skills allowing you to adapt them for your current class topics.

Using the activities
Each activity is broken down into the areas outlined below.

Age Range
This section highlights the recommended age range for each particular game. Within each chapter, there are examples of games covering different age ranges, enabling teachers to get a good curricular cover for both primary age levels.

Learning Objectives
The learning objective sets out the intended outcome of each game and relates to the relevant Government guidelines of the NC, QCA, NLS or the NNS.

Curriculum Links
This section will help you to quickly find direct links to the relevant Government documents such as the National Curriculum and the QCA, where applicable. These links can help you with your planning and assessment and with the development of ideas for future relevant activities.

What you need
In this section you will find a clear, concise list of the resources needed for each game. As the games last for just 10 minutes, the resources needed for most of them are minimal and easy to obtain within the school environment, and many simply require a safe, open space such as a large room or hall. A few of the games may need resources made in advance, but once made, the games can be played with little or no preparation. Some games use photocopiable sheets for items such as game boards and game cards, and these can be found at the end of each chapter. Due to time and cost, these have been kept to a minimum. If possible, laminate the game boards and playing cards once you have photocopied them, and store the resources so that they are easily accessible for future use.

What to do
This section gives a step-by-step explanation of how to play the game. Before it is played, it is important to set the game in context so that the children understand what they are trying to achieve and what skills they are trying to learn. With this in mind, each game starts off with examples of questions or ideas for brief discussions on the game's specific objective. The games are set out in straightforward bullet points followed by examples of ways in which you can reflect on the game to help consolidate the skills that the children have learned.

Where applicable, the size of the playing group is highlighted, but most of the games can be adapted to be played in pairs, small groups or whole-class groups.

Differentiation
At the end of each game you will find a 'Differentiation' section. This provides suggestions for ways in which you can adapt a game to support younger or less able children, or extend it to challenge older or more able children.

Safety
Specific safety pointers have been given throughout the book, but, as with any of your daily activities, consider safety aspects and potential hazards before you carry out any of the games.

The value of play
All types of educational games encourage skills in thinking, dealing with relationships, teamwork and learning new ideas and concepts. The versatility and enjoyment of a fun 10-minute game has a strong and popular place within the school curriculum, and long may it last.

CHAPTER 1

English

AGE RANGE 5–7

LEARNING OBJECTIVE
To listen to adults giving detailed explanations and presentations.

CURRICULUM LINKS
KS1: En1 2a, 2b, 2e, 9b.
NLS: Y2 T1 Text 17.

Origami challenge

What you need
A4 paper; paper squares measuring 30cm by 30cm; the 'Origami challenge – Aeroplane' and 'Origami challenge – Hat' photocopiable sheets on pages 17 and 18.

What to do
● Encourage the children to think about occasions when they need to listen and concentrate. Offer examples, such as crossing the road or following simple oral instructions to build something.
● Tell the children that you are going to show them how to make a simple origami model. Ask whether anyone knows what the word origami means. If necessary, explain that it is an ancient Japanese art of folding paper to make different models.
● Explain that you would like the children to listen carefully and copy your instructions as you make a model.
● Give each child one piece of A4 paper. Using the 'Origami challenge – Aeroplane' photocopiable sheet, make an origami model of an aeroplane. Talk through the stages clearly, for example, *First, fold your piece of paper lengthwise.*
● Show your finished aeroplane to the class. Check that the children were able to listen and follow your instructions by holding up their aeroplanes and testing them to see if they fly.
● Next, using the 'Origami challenge – Hat' photocopiable sheet, encourage the children to watch you make another origami model. Explain that, this time, they cannot make their model until you have finished yours.
● Encourage the children to watch, listen and remember the different steps to make an origami paper hat.
● When you have finished, give each child a sheet of paper and challenge them to make a model hat in less than three minutes.
● After three minutes, shout *Stop!* Look at the hats that have been completed correctly. Ask those children how they remembered how to make the model. Did they remember specific points? Did they look at it visually to see where the next fold went? Invite them to talk about their strategy to the rest of the group.

Differentiation
Highlight your use of instructional language as you show younger children what to do. Older or more able children can try out more complicated origami patterns. For a variation of the game, put the children into small mixed-ability groups. Give everyone a sheet of paper and give an origami pattern to one child in each group. This child should give clear instructions for making the origami model to the rest of the group.

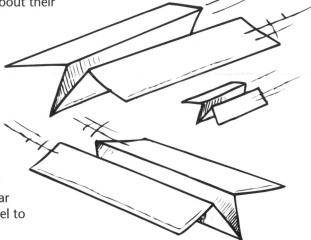

Alphabetical shopping

AGE RANGE 5–7

LEARNING OBJECTIVE
To practise and secure alphabetic letter knowledge and alphabetic order.

CURRICULUM LINKS
KS1: En1 1b, 2a, 2f, 3a; En2 1b, 1c.
NLS: Y1, T1, Word 2; Y1, T2, Word 1; Y2, T3, Word 1.

What you need
A clear floor space; alphabet frieze or poster; a timer with a second hand.

What to do
● Display the alphabet frieze or chart where the children can see it. Invite everyone to sit in a circle to play an alphabet game.
● Explain that a big shopping centre has just been built. Encourage the children to think of different shops that could be in the shopping centre such as a toy shop, clothes shop and tool shop.
● Start the game by saying that you are going to think of a character beginning with the letter *a*, who is shopping for something beginning with the same letter. For example, you could say: *I am an alien and I want to buy an apple.*
● Still using the letter a, invite the child on your left to continue the game by offering their own character and object, for example: *I am an archer and I want to buy an arrow.*
● Continue around the circle until you call out *Change*. Depending on the skill of the group, you may also want to call out or point to the next alphabetical letter.
● The next child should then think of a character and object beginning with b, for example: *I am a baby and I want to buy a bib.*
● If children who are struggling, encourage them to ask their neighbours for help. If they still cannot think of a character and object, invite them to move on to the next letter.
● At the end of the game, discuss which were the hardest and easiest letters to use.
● Highlight some of the shoppers and their items. Suggest that the children could use them as a basis for a short story or a fun poem.

Differentiation
Provide picture prompts for younger children. Encourage more able children to use adjectives and adverbs in the game. For example, *The anxious ant wanted to buy an amazing ant city.* For an alternative game, invite the children to tell a story as they work around the circle, with each child contributing a sentence using the next alphabetical letter.

10-Minute Games

BRIGHT IDEAS

AGE RANGE 5–7

LEARNING OBJECTIVE
To put a text into a correct sequence in order for it to make sense.

CURRICULUM LINKS
KS1: En2 1k, 1l, 1m, 1n, 3b, 4.
NLS: Y1, T1, Sentence 1; Y1, T3, Text 5; Y2, T1, Text 4.

Sequencing relays

What you need
Copies of a comic strip story with the storyline or sequence cut up into pieces (one set for each team); one intact comic strip story; a safe, open space.

What to do
● Show the children a story from a comic. Help them to notice that each picture in the comic strip is in the correct sequence. Explain that the term sequence is another word for order. Ask the children what would happen if the comic strip was not in the correct sequence.

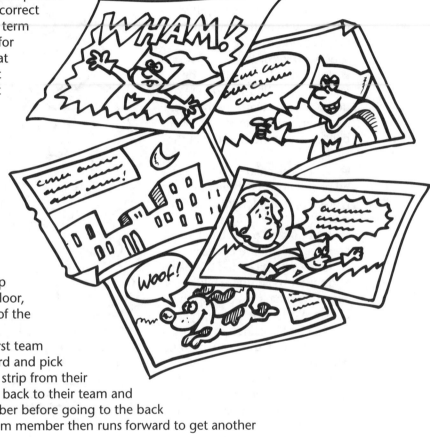

● Introduce the game, explaining that the children are going to play a sequencing relay game with a difference.
● Organise the children into teams of five or six. Ask the teams to stand in a line behind a fixed starting point.
● Place each pile of cut up comic-strip pieces on the floor, about five metres in front of the teams.
● On the word *Go*, the first team member should run forward and pick up one piece of the comic strip from their pile. They should then run back to their team and touch the next team member before going to the back of the line. The second team member then runs forward to get another piece of comic strip.
● Depending on the size of the team and the number of comic strip pieces, some members may need to run twice.
● Once all of the comic strip pieces have been collected, the teams have to put the pieces into the correct sequence.
● The team who gets the correct sequence first wins.
● At the end of the game, look at the main clues in the comic strip that helped the teams to put the pieces in the correct sequence. Highlight the way that the pictures, dialogue, settings, actions and responses of characters could all be clues.

Differentiation
For less able children, use photocopied pages from a short and familiar text, and ask them to put the pages in the correct sequence. For more able children, use non-fiction text that follows a set format or formal layout. For example, letters, newspaper front pages or instructions.

AGE RANGE 5-11

LEARNING OBJECTIVE
To understand that antonyms are words with opposite meanings and to look at different types of antonyms.

CURRICULUM LINKS
KS1: En1 1b, 2a, 3a; En3 1a.
NLS: Y2, T2, Word 11; Y3, T1 Word 11.

The opposites game

What you need
A clear floor space; tennis ball (or a large soft ball for younger and less able children).

What to do
● Invite the children to sit in a large circle to play an 'opposites' game. Say a word, such as *large*, to the group and ask the children what they think the opposite word could be. They might suggest *small* or *little*.
● Introduce the game to the children. Explain that you are going to say a word, such as *in*, and then you are going to roll a ball to one of the children in the circle.
● When the child gets the ball, he or she must say the opposite word, for example, *out*. They must then think of a new word, such as *up*, and roll the ball to another child in the circle.
● Once they have had the ball and sent it to another child, they can cross their arms to stop the ball coming to them again.
● If a child does not know an opposite word, they can ask their neighbours for help.
● If they still cannot think of the word, they should roll the ball to someone else and cross their arms.
● Continue playing the game until everyone in the circle is crossing their arms.
● At the end of the game, recap the words that came up. Explain to the children that words that mean the opposite to other words are called *antonyms*.

Differentiation
Provide extra adult support in the circle for groups of younger children. For older or more able children, use the game to investigate antonyms of a more advanced vocabulary and word meaning such as *rude/polite* and *love/hate*. Alternatively, focus on the examples of prefixes in antonyms such as *happy/unhappy*, *appear/disappear* and *ordinary/extraordinary*.

AGE RANGE 7–8

LEARNING OBJECTIVE
To identify how character and setting are created, and how plot, narrative structure and themes develop.

CURRICULUM LINKS
KS2: En1 1b, 1d, 2e, 4a; En2 4c, 4e.
NLS: Y3, T1, Text 1; Y4, T1, Text 4.

Lucky dip stories

What you need
The 'Lucky dip – characters' and 'Lucky dip – settings' photocopiable sheets on pages 19 and 20 (photocopy and cut out two or three sets of cards depending on your group size); two boxes labelled 'Characters' and 'Settings'; pens; paper.

What to do
● Talk about story structure with the children. Explain that, when planning a story, it can help if you decide on the setting and characters before you start to think of the plot.
● Talk about different genre of stories, such as adventure stories, traditional tales, mystery stories and comical stories.
● Introduce the game, explaining that the children are going to work in groups of three to make up a story with a given genre, such as a space adventure, using two settings and two main character cards.
● Put each set of cards into the labelled boxes. Ask one child from each group to pick two cards from the 'Character' box and two from the 'Settings' box.
● Give each group a pen and paper, and ask the children to appoint a scribe to make notes on the story structure.
● Tell the children that they can make up two additional minor characters for their story if necessary.
● Remind them that their stories need a clear beginning, middle and end, then invite each group to make up a story using the given genre and their character and setting cards for inspiration.
● After three minutes, ask each group to stand up and tell or perform their story to the rest of the class.
● When all of the stories have been told, vote on the overall favourite.
● Discuss briefly what it was that the children liked so much about that particular story. How did it start? How did the winning group incorporate the characters and settings? What happened in the story to keep it interesting? How did it end?

Differentiation
Less able children could play the game as individuals within a small group. Provide a story beginning (made up or well-known) then, in turn, let the children choose a character and continue the story where it was left by the previous player. Give the story an ending. Encourage more able children to think about the story structure. Explain that many stories have a dilemma that the characters try to resolve. Look at openings and endings of stories and give the children a set opening or ending at the beginning of the game.

AGE RANGE 7–8

LEARNING OBJECTIVE
To investigate and use speech bubbles to reinforce a storyline.

CURRICULUM LINKS
KS2: En1 4a, 4b, 4d, 6a, 6c; En2 2c; En3 1a, 7b.
NLS: Y3, T1, Sentence 9, Text 2, 13; Y3, T3, Text 10; Y4 T1, Text 4.

Speech bubble mimes

What you need
A safe, open space; whiteboard or flipchart; pens; scissors; blank paper; a written title of a short narrative such as the tale 'The boy who cried wolf' or a well-known poem such as 'The Owl and the Pussy cat', for each group.

What to do
● Draw a large speech bubble on the board or chart and ask the children what it is. Explain that speech bubbles can show what someone is saying or doing within a text.
● Write out different types of text that can be put inside a speech bubble. For example, one-word speech bubbles used to emphasise an action or emotion such as *Pull!*, *Great!* or *Jump!*; or a sentence speech bubble to highlight key notions or actions such as *Where am I?* or *The queen must be stopped!*

● Invite the children to play a miming game. Organise them into groups of four or five and give each group six blank pieces of paper, pens, scissors and a written example of a short narrative.
● Explain that each group has one minute to perform a mime of the fable or poem to the other groups. Although they are not allowed to talk, the groups can use up to six speech bubbles to help reinforce the fable or poem.
● Emphasise the need to think carefully about what should be written in the speech bubbles and how they are going to be used throughout the mime.
● Give the children three minutes to prepare their mime and speech cards, then invite one of the groups to perform their mime.
● When they have finished, challenge the other groups to guess what the story could be, picking up clues from the mime and the speech bubbles.
● Repeat with the remaining groups of children.
● At the end of the game, talk about and categorise the different types of speech bubbles used by the groups.

Differentiation
Work with smaller groups of less able children and give each group a single scene to mime. Encourage the groups to perform each scene in sequence. Older and more able children could mime their own choice of stories. To make the game more of a challenge, choose a book that the children are familiar with, and give them a chapter or story section each. At the end of the mimes, ask the class to put their mimes into the correct sequence.

AGE RANGE 7–11

LEARNING OBJECTIVE
To broaden vocabulary and to use words in inventive ways.

CURRICULUM LINKS
KS2: En3 1b, 1c.
NLS: Y5, T2, Sentence 7, 8.

Acrostic codes

What you need
Paper; pens or pencils; whiteboard or flipchart.

What to do
● Explain that an acrostic is a puzzle in which the first letters of each line spell a word or a sentence. Write a simple word such as *MATHS* on the whiteboard or flipchart. Invite the children to help you write the word out as an acrostic puzzle, for example: *My Apple Tastes Horribly Sour*.

● Invite the children to play a game. Organise them into groups of up to four and explain that they are going to make up a code using acrostics.

● Tell the children that you will give the groups a word, such as *CHAIR*, and a name or subject, such as an *ASTRONAUT*.

● The groups should then make up an acrostic message using the word *CHAIR*, which is from or about an *ASTRONAUT*. The words of the message must start with the letters of *CHAIR* in their correct order. So, for example, they might write *Call Headquarters! Aliens In Raid*.

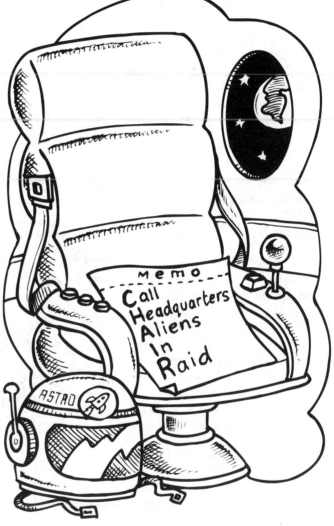

● To begin the game, choose any type of word, such as a noun, verb or adjective, and a fictional or factual subject, such as aliens or dinosaurs. You could also choose any character such as a pirate or firefighter, a famous person such as Queen Victoria or a fictional character such as The BFG.

● Give the groups two minutes to work out a message. After two minutes, invite each group to read out their code. Ask each group to explain how they thought of their ideas, then take a vote on the favourite code.

● Invite the winning group to suggest another word and subject or name, then play the game again.

Differentiation
For less able children, give them a three- or four-letter word such as *HAT*. Encourage them to use the first letters of the word to make up a phrase or a sentence on a particular theme, such as 'animals'. For example, they could say *Horses Are Tall*. Encourage more able children to make up acrostic codes using longer and more complicated words, such as *RHYTHM* or *DICTIONARY*.

AGE RANGE 7–11

LEARNING OBJECTIVE
To form long sentences with restricted word length, using connecting words and devices.

CURRICULUM LINKS
KS2: En2 4b, 6; En3 1b, 3, 7b, 7c.
NLS: Y3, T3, Sentence 5; Y4, T2, Sentence 12; Y5, T1, Sentence 3; Y5, T2, Sentence 8; Y5, T3, Sentence 6, 7; Y6, T1, Sentence 4, 5.

Fun sentences

What you need
Paper; pens; whiteboard or flipchart.

What to do
● On the board or flipchart, write a sentence with words that are no more than four letters long. For example, *Sita and Nick ran very fast and got to the bus stop just in time.*
● Ask the children what they notice about the words in the sentence. Highlight the length of each word.
● Invite the children to play a game. Explain that they have to write the longest sentence they can, using words with up to four letters.
● Before they begin, discuss ways in which they can make a long sentence. Talk about the use of lists, and commas within lists. Look briefly at connectives such as *if*, *so*, *while* and *since*, and how to use connectives to link clauses within sentences.
● Distribute the pens and paper among the children.
● Tell the children that they now have four minutes to make as many long sentences as they can. Explain that their sentences can be fun and silly.
● At the end of the four minutes, ask each child in turn to read out his or her longest sentence to the class. Write them on the board as the children read them out.

● Count the words in each sentence to find the winner. To make the game more fun, encourage the children to try to read out their sentences in one breath!
● At the end of the game, talk about the use of connectives and lists. Discuss how hard it is to think of words that have just four letters or less.

Differentiation
For younger and less able children, give them a list of word families. Write the words on the board, for example: bat; cat; fat; hat; mat; pat; rat; sat; tat; vat. Ask the children to make a long sentence using as many of the listed words as they can. Encourage more able children to write long sentences using words of just three letters. For example, *The shy old hen got her new red hat and let the boy eat the top for his tea.* For more of a challenge, allow the children to use just one connective within the sentence, or no connectives at all.

10–Minute Games

AGE RANGE 7–11

LEARNING OBJECTIVE
To use a range of reading and spelling strategies to unravel jumbled letters.

CURRICULUM LINKS
KS2: En2 1b, 2a; En3 4a, 4c, 4d, 4j.
NLS: Y3, T3, Word 6, Sentence 1; Y4-6 Word 3; Y6, T1-3, Word 6.

Jumbled

What you need
A whiteboard or flipchart; paper; pens; timer with a second hand.

What to do
● Prior to the session, prepare a list of words that can be jumbled up. The words can be on any topic, such as famous people, books, countries, animals or any other topic that your class is currently studying.
● Introduce the game to the children. Explain that you are going to give them some jumbled up words relating to your chosen topic. They have to un-jumble the letters to find the correct words.
● Write a jumbled word on the board, for example: *eadrb* (bread) or *plbateha* (alphabet).
● Briefly discuss ways of finding the proper words. For example, you could look for letter patterns such as *br* or *ea*, the vowels, think about the length and the shape of the words, or look for capital letters.
● Place the children in mixed ability pairs and give each pair a pen and paper.
● Write out the first jumbled word on the board. As you write, give the children a clue by explaining the topic that your word has been taken from. For example: a famous person from the past: *yMra leScaoe* (Mary Seacole).
● In their pairs, challenge the children to work out the jumbled word.
● Once a pair think they have worked out the word, they should put their hands up and everyone else should stop working.
● If they are correct, the pair get one point. If they are wrong, the class continues working until a pair gets the correct word.
● The game then continues with another jumbled word. At the end of the session, the pair with the most points are the winners.

Differentiation
For younger and less able children, concentrate on three- to four-letter words with common letter patterns. For example, write the jumbled word *ornbw* and explain that it is a colour with the letter patterns *br* or *ow* in it. For more able children extend one or two jumbled words into a jumbled sentence such as a well-known saying. They could also look at a range of complex words with unusual letter patterns such as *rhythmic* or *hypothermia*.

AGE RANGE 8–11

LEARNING OBJECTIVE
To be aware of and understand the meanings of phrases, expressions and proverbs.

CURRICULUM LINKS
KS2: En2 2a, 2b, 2c, 4a, 6; En3 7c.
NLS: Y5, T1, Word 9; Y5, T2, Word 12; Y6, T2, Word 6.

How does it end?

What you need
The 'How does it end? Phrases and sayings' and 'How does it end? Proverbs' photocopiable sheets on pages 21 and 22; pens or pencils.

What to do
● Depending on the knowledge and skills of your class the phrases and proverbs sheets can be used in one or two ten-minute game sessions.

Phrases and sayings
● Organise the children into pairs. Explain that they are going to play a game in which they have to complete phrases and sayings.
● Give an example of one phrase, such as *Like a fish out of water*. Ask the children what they think the phrase means. Notice how the first part of the phrase can be a clue to the last part.
● Give each pair a copy of the 'How does it end? Phrases and sayings' photocopiable sheet. Explain that the children have five minutes to work together to write the missing word or words in the appropriate spaces. If any of the pairs finish the phrases before the end of five minutes, challenge them to make up a few of their own.
● At the end of five minutes, let the children mark their work as you read out the correct answers. Ask the meaning of each one as you go through the list.

Proverbs
● Explain to the children that a proverb is a short sentence concerning a truth or a moral about something or someone.
● Notice that a proverb has its main subject at the beginning and the result or moral at the end.
● Still in their pairs, give the class five minutes to work out the proverbs on the 'How does it end? Proverbs' photocopiable sheet.
● At the end of the game, discuss the meaning of each proverb.

Answers
Phrases and sayings: new pin; hatter; mule; bull; flame; slaughter; black; wrong foot; drain/hyena; log; hills; lark; boots; lead; new-born baby.

Proverbs: no moss; no man; a rest; not gold; a thousand words; you come to it; who wait; it pours; best medicine; run deep; fire; better than one; the sword; you eat.

Differentiation
Tell less able children the first part of a simple saying or phrase and give them three possible answers to choose from. For example, *As brave as a …? Is it a robot, lion or snake?* Give more able children the end words or word and challenge them to work out the first part of the phrases or proverbs.

Origami challenge

Aeroplane

1 Fold a piece of A4 paper lengthways down the middle and open out.

2 Fold the top corners down to the middle line.

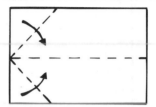

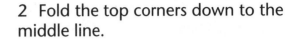

3 Fold the top parts of the plane down, creasing along the middle of the paper.

4 Fold the top corners to the middle line. Make sure the point is still showing.

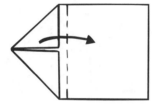

5 Fold the point of the aeroplane backwards.

6 Fold the plane lengthways.

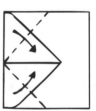

7 Fold the wings down on both sides.

8 Fold out wings and see if the aeroplane can fly!

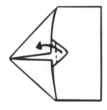

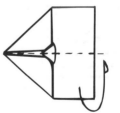

Origami challenge

Hat

1　Take a square piece of paper and fold in half lengthways.

2　Fold in edges on both sides to meet in the middle.

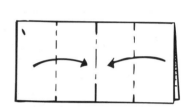

3　Fold top corner out to the edges.

4　Pull out the top part of each section then fold back the sides.

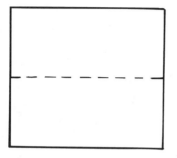

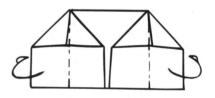

5　Fold up the bottom parts three times in 1/2cm sections.

6　Do the same on the other side.

7　Pull out the middle section to get the hat shape.

SCHOLASTIC

Lucky dip stories – characters

Lucky dip stories – settings

How does it end?

Phrases and sayings

1. Shining like a _____

2. As mad as a _____

3. As stubborn as a _____

4. Like a red rag to a _____

5. Like a moth to a _____

6. Like a lamb to the _____

7. The pot calling the kettle _____

8. Get off on the _____

9. Laugh like a _____

10. To sleep like a _____

11. As old as the _____

12. Singing like a _____

13. Too big for their _____

14. As heavy as _____

15. As innocent as a _____

How does it end?

Proverbs

1. A rolling stone gathers _____

2. Time and tide wait for _____

3. A change is as good as _____

4. All that glisters is _____

5. A picture paints _____

6. Don't cross the bridge until _____

7. Good things come to those _____

8. It never rains but _____

9. Laughter is the _____

10. Still waters _____

11. There's no smoke without _____

12. Two heads are _____

13. The pen is mightier than _____

14. You are what _____.

10–Minute Games

BRIGHT IDEAS

CHAPTER 2

Maths

AGE RANGE 5–7

LEARNING OBJECTIVE
To know and use units of time and the relationships between them.

CURRICULUM LINKS
KS1: Ma3 4a.
NNS: Measures (Y1–3, p78-79).

Paper cup towers

What you need
Paper cups; a timer showing seconds and minutes; whiteboard or flip chart.

What to do
● Begin by explaining that there are sixty seconds in one minute. Ask the children to count out sixty seconds.
● Now do two sets of sixty seconds, counting: 1, 2, 3... 58, 59 one minute; 1,2, 3... 58, 59, two minutes. Tell the children that they have just counted out two minutes.
● Invite the children to play a game. Organise them into teams of three or four. Explain that each team has to build a tower with paper cups. They can build the tower in any shape they like, but they have just two minutes in which to do it.
● Ask the children to estimate how many cups they think they might be able to balance in two minutes. Explain that balancing paper cups can be quite difficult and the towers may fall over several times. Write down each team's estimations on a board.
● Put the groups in different parts of the room and distribute the paper cups. Give the children one minute to discuss ideas and strategies.
● On the word *Go* start the timer and let the children start building their cup towers.
● Call out the time after one minute, then at the end of two minutes tell everyone to stop.
● Invite each team to count the cups in their tower. The winner is the team with the most cups in a standing tower. Which team got the nearest to their estimated number of cups?
● Start the game again but this time ask the children to estimate how many cups they think they will use in just one minute.
● Write out their estimations on the board and start the game.
● Each team can appoint someone to silently count the seconds so they know how long they have. Stop the teams after one minute and count the cups.
● Look at the estimates again. Ask the children if the estimates were closer this time and why.

Differentiation
Work with pairs of younger children and provide adult support to balance the cups as the tower gets higher. Give older or more able children more complicated challenges such as a playing card tower. Ask them to estimate, to the exact minute and seconds, how long it would take to make a playing card tower using a set amount of cards.

AGE RANGE 5–7

LEARNING OBJECTIVE
To add two or three single-digit numbers mentally.

CURRICULUM LINKS
KS1: MA2 2a.
NNS: Understanding addition and subtraction (Y1–3, p26–27).

Robot by numbers

What you need
The 'Robot by numbers' photocopiable sheet on page 33; dice; plain paper; pencils; rulers.

What to do
● Arrange the children in pairs or small groups.

● Before beginning the game, discuss different combinations of numbers that could be thrown using three dice. Notice that the same total can come from different number combinations. For example, 1 + 3 + 2, 2 + 2 + 2 and 4 + 1 + 1 make 6. Explain that the highest number total of three dice is 18 (6 + 6 + 6).

● Introduce the game to the children. Explain that they are going to design a robot according to the numbers that they throw using three dice.

● Give three dice and a copy of the 'Robot by numbers' photocopiable sheet to each group, and paper, pencil and ruler to each child.

● In turn, let the children throw all three dice and add up the numbers to give them a total number. Encourage them to try to mentally calculate the numbers on the dice.

● They will need to look at the photocopiable sheet to see which part of their robot they can draw. For example, if they get a total of five, they can draw a head. They can design whatever robot they like, as long as they put in the correct number of design features. If they already have, for example, two eyes, they should pass the dice to the next player.

● The winner is the first player to finish their robot.

Differentiation
Play the game as a class activity with younger or less able children. Let each child in turn roll the dice and call out the numbers. The children should work out the total and then put up their hands to give you the answer. The child with the correct answer can draw the part of the robot, and the game ends when the robot is finished. Use four or five dice for older or more able children. Ask them to think of ways that they can mentally add the five numbers together. You could also make dice with two-digit numbers on them to encourage addition of larger numbers.

AGE RANGE 5–7

LEARNING OBJECTIVE
To use the +, - and = signs to record mental additions and subtractions in a number sentence.

CURRICULUM LINKS
KS1: Ma2 1e, 1f, 3a.
NNS: Understanding addition and subtraction (Y1–3, p24–29).

Heads up, numbers up

What you need
Number cards from 1 to 20 (choose your own range of number cards to match the ability of your group); three large cards showing a +, – and = sign; paper; pencils; whiteboard or flipchart.

What to do
● Give each child a sheet of paper and a pencil. Show the children the +, – and = sign cards and discuss what each means.
● On the board, write an example of a addition number sentence, such as 3 + 7 = 10, and a subtraction number sentence, such as 7 – 3 = 4.
● Invite the children to play a game. Explain that they are going to make addition and subtraction number sentences.
● Give a number card to each child. Tell the children to look at them and then put them down on the table in front of them.
● Next, ask the children to lay their heads on top of their cards and hold their thumbs up. Go around the class and touch the thumbs of four children, then go back to the front and say *Heads up, numbers up.*
● The four children whose thumbs have been touched should come up to the front and hold up their number cards. Ask the children to say the numbers as you write them out on the board, for example: 4, 7, 10, 15.
● Challenge the children to make up two addition sentences and two subtraction sentences using the numbers on the board as the totals. For example: 5 + 2 = 7; 6 + 4 = 10; 8 – 4 = 4; 20 – 5 = 15.
● When the children have made up their four number sentences, encourage them to put their hands up. Write the different examples on the board.
● Start the game again by asking the children to put their heads down and thumbs up. Let the four children from the previous round touch a thumb each. When the next four children have brought their cards to the front and the last four have sat down, you can begin the game again.

Differentiation
Less able children can concentrate on just addition sentences or subtraction sentences. Give them three numbers within their ability range with which to make their sentences. Older or more able children could make up addition and subtraction sums using larger numbers in the tens, hundreds, thousands and so on.

AGE RANGE 5–8

LEARNING OBJECTIVE
To create and describe number patterns.

CURRICULUM LINKS
KS1 and KS2: MA2 2b.
NNS: Counting, properties of numbers and number sequences (Y1–3, p4-7).

Next in line

What you need
Number patterns on separate pieces of paper (see below), pencils; paper.

What to do
● Organise the children into teams of five or six. Give each team a piece of paper with number instructions to make up a number sequence. For example: *A number pattern of even numbers; A number pattern which has the numbers 7 and 16 in it; A number pattern using the number 5.*
● The children have to use the number patterns to create a number sequence using any numbers they want. For example, an even sequence could be 2, 4, 6, 8, 10, 12 or a number sequence which has the numbers 7 and 16 in it could be 2, 4, 7, 11, 16, 22.
● The amount of numbers in each sequence should be the same as the number of players in the team, for example, six numbers in a team of six. The teams must also work out the next number in the sequence, so that they can challenge the other teams to work out their number sequence.
● Give the teams up to two minutes to decide on their sequences. After two minutes, invite the teams to take turns to stand up. Each player in the team should call out a number from their sequence in the correct order.
● The other teams have up to one minute to work together to decide on the next number in the sequence.
● Encourage the teams to put up their hands when they think they know the answer. If they are correct, they get one team point. If they are incorrect, ask the next team who put their hands up.
● For a bonus point, ask them to tell you what the number pattern is and how they worked it out.
● Now ask another team to come up and call out their number sequence.
● Once all of the teams have called out their sequences, count up the points. The winner is the team with the most points.

Differentiation
Work with smaller groups of younger children. Older or more able children could create their own number patterns within the one-minute time limit. Encourage them to create number patterns by adding and subtracting numbers in the same sequence. They could also create sequences that extend beyond zero and use negative numbers.

AGE RANGE 7–8

LEARNING OBJECTIVE
Recognise simple fractions that are several parts of one whole.

CURRICULUM LINKS
KS2: Ma2 2d.
NNS: Fractions (Y3, p21–23; Y4, p22–26).

Fraction pizzas

What you need
The 'Fraction pizzas 1' and 'Fractions pizzas 2' photocopiable sheets on pages 34 and 35.

What to do
● Before the game, use the photocopiable sheets to prepare some sets of pizza cards, depending on the abilities of your children. Prepare enough cards so that each child can make at least two complete pizzas. Divide and label the pizza on the 'Fractions pizzas 2' sheet according your children's abilities, for example, into thirds for younger children and tenths for more able children.

● Introduce the game. Tell the children that they have to make complete pizzas from individual slices.

● Show the children one of the pizzas with its slices still in place. Ask them how many slices are in the pizza and, together, name the fraction numbers on each slice.

● Organise the children into small groups. Give each group a set of shuffled slice cards and put them face down in a pile in front of the children.

● In turn, invite the children to take a pizza card from the pile. This forms the first piece of their pizza. Continue playing, challenging the children to collect the other fractions to make a complete pizza. If they turn over a fraction that they need for their pizza, they should put the card in the correct place. If they already have that fraction, they should put the card in a new pile, face down, and let the next child take a turn.

● They must complete one whole pizza before they can move on and collect another.

● Once the first pile of slices has been turned over, the new pile is shuffled and the game continues.

● When all of the slices have gone, the players should count their complete pizzas. The winner is the player with the most complete pizzas with the fraction pieces in the correct order.

Differentiation
For younger or less able children, play the game in two teams in a large space. Each team have pizza slice cut-outs, mixed up and placed face down on the floor. On the word *Go*, the children have to collect the slices and make them into whole pizzas with the fractions in the correct order. The first team to have all the pizzas with the slices in the correct order are the winners. More able children can make up pizzas using decimal fractions and recognising the equivalent fractions.

What's my number?

AGE RANGE 7–11

LEARNING OBJECTIVE
To recall and recognise multiplication facts to 10 x 10.

CURRICULUM LINKS
KS2: Ma2 2b, 3f, 3h.
NNS: Rapid recall of multiplication and division facts (Y3–6, p58–59).

What you need
Multiplication question cards (see below; enough for one per child); corresponding answer cards; a safe open space.

What to do
● Before you start the game, choose two or three multiplication tables appropriate to your children's abilities, for example, the 3-, 5- and 7-times tables.

● Prepare the question and answer cards. Write out a mix of question styles such as *Nine fives is …*; *4 × 6*; *5 multiplied by 5*; *Multiply 8 by 4*. Write the corresponding answers on a separate set of cards.

● Introduce the game to the children. Explain that you are going to give a multiplication card to each child, and that you will put the answer cards face down on the floor. Tell the children what your two or three chosen multiplication tables are.

● On the word *Go*, invite all of the children to turn over the answer cards to find the solution to their multiplication card.

● If they turn over an incorrect card, they must turn it back over again and continue looking. If they think they have found the correct answer, they must find other children from the same multiplication table.

● When all of the children from a multiplication table have found their cards, they must put themselves in the correct order. If there is a wrong answer, the child should go back and find the correct answer.

● Once a team has all the correct answers in the correct sequence they must put up their hands.

● At the end of the game, ask each team in finishing order to stand up and say their multiplication table to the rest of the class.

● The winners are the first team to finish with the correct order of answers.

Differentiation
Younger children could investigate odd and even number sequences. Put out number cards face down on the floor and organise the children into odd and even teams. Challenge them to turn over the cards to find the correct number for their teams. For older and more able children, use the game to investigate division facts. Give out division questions such as *36 divided by 3* and *15 divided by 3*. The children have to find the answers and join others with same divisible number.

AGE RANGE 7–11

LEARNING OBJECTIVE
To choose suitable number operations to solve a given problem.

CURRICULUM LINKS
KS2: Ma2 1b, 3a.
NNS: Pencil and paper procedures (Y4–6, p48–51, 66–69).

Climb the mountains

What you need
The 'Climb the Mountains' photocopiable sheet on page 36 (you can also use a mountain outline with other mountain heights); pencils; paper.

What to do
● This game can be played individually, in pairs or in groups. The aim is to be the first player or group to reach the peak of the highest mountain (Mount Everest).
● Show the children the mountain peaks outline from the photocopiable sheet. Point out that the lowest peak, Ben Nevis, is in Great Britain and is 1343m high.
● Ask the children what the next highest peak is. (Mount Cook in New Zealand, which is 3746m high.)
● Explain to the children that they have to make sums using the four single digit numbers in 1343 to get to the total of 3746. Explain that they can add, subtract, multiply or divide the numbers and they can use the numbers more than once.
● Go through the first part with the children. For example, 1343 × 3 = 4029; 4029 – 313 = 3716; 3716 + 34 = 3750; 3750 – 4 = 3746. Tell the children that each sum is like a step forward or backward towards the target number, as if they are climbing up a challenging mountain.
● Encourage the children to write out each sum step until the total number is reached.
● The winner is the first player, pair or group to reach the peak of Mount Everest.
● After the game, talk about the different sums used by the children. Discuss which was the easiest peak and the hardest peaks to climb and why.

Differentiation
Younger or less able children could investigate numbers using 100s, 10s and units. Encourage them to make up sums to go up ladder steps or a beanstalk from *Jack and the Beanstalk*. More able children could play the game using other large numbers in the 1000s, 100s, 10s, and units such as river lengths. They could also try to cross the nine planets using sums into the 100,000s.

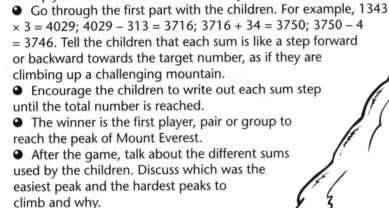

AGE RANGE 7–11

LEARNING OBJECTIVE
To find totals in money and give change.

CURRICULUM LINKS
KS2: Ma2 3e, 4a.
NNS: Problems involving 'real life' money or measures
(Y1–3, p69; Y4–6, p84–85).

Small change

What you need
A hall; two amounts of the same change such as two pounds' worth of 1p, 2p, 5p, 10p, 20p, 50p; four chairs.

What to do
● Show the children an amount of small change. Pose some addition and subtraction questions. For example, *Which coins can I use to make up a total of £1.77?*; *If I have £1.99, which coins should I take away to get 80p?*.
● Invite the children to play a game. Organise them into two equal teams and number them so that each team has corresponding numbers of players.
● Place two chairs at one end of the hall and explain that these represent the shops. Place two more chairs at the opposite end of the hall and explain that these represent the banks. Each team has a shop chair and a bank chair.

Coins © The Royal Mint

● Put an equal amount of small change coins on both the bank chairs.
● Invite the children to sit in their number sequence at the side of the hall between their two chairs. Begin the game by calling out an amount of money to be taken from the bank to the shop, and a team player number.
● The players who have been allocated that number in each team must run to the bank chair and pick up the correct amount of change. They should then run to the shop chair, and count out aloud the correct small change to be left 'in the shop'.
● The first player back in the team line, after choosing the correct amount of small change, receives a team point.
● Continue playing, with another amount of change and two more players.
● These players now have to remember how much change is already on the shop chair and add to it or take money away from it to get the next correct amount. Make sure there are enough correct coins for them to use.
● The winners are the team with the most points.

Differentiation
Younger or less able children can use a small amount of small change coins such as 1p, 2p, 5p and 10p. Choose simple amounts for them to count out such as 25p and then 30p (add another 5p). Older or more able children can use notes for larger sums of money, and mentally calculate more challenging amounts such as £12. 65 then £4.24 (take away change of £8.41).

AGE RANGE 8–11

LEARNING OBJECTIVE
To recognise geometrical features and properties of shapes, lines and angles.
To recognise and use geometrical language.

CURRICULUM LINKS
KS2: Ma3 2a, 2b.
NNS: Shape and space (Y4–6, pp. 102–103, 108–109, 110–111).

Geometry bingo

What you need
The 'Geometry bingo – picture cards' and 'Geometry bingo – word cards' photocopiable sheets on pages 37 and 38 (enlarged and cut into individual cards); whiteboard; Blu-tack.

What to do
● Prepare for the game by writing the geometric names on the back of the picture cards.
● Invite the children to play a game of 'Geometric bingo'. Explain that the aim of the game is to match the geometric name or terms with the correct geometric picture.
● Stick the picture cards on a whiteboard or at the front of the class so that everyone can see them. Explain that you are going to call out a geometric name to each team, and they have to decide which picture matches the name.
● As an example, say *Parallelogram*. Ask the children what properties make up a parallelogram (it has opposite sides that are equal and parallel). Challenge the children to point to the picture that matches those properties.
● Organise the children into two or four teams. Choose one team to begin, and call out a geometric name or term from the fword cards. After conferring, one of the team members should come to the front, explain the characteristics of that particular geometric shape, and stick the name card on top of the picture that they think it matches.
● If they are correct, that team scores one point.
● If they are incorrect, they do not get a point and a new name is called out to the next team.
● When all of the pictures have been covered up, count up the points to find the winning team.
● After the game, highlight any particular geometric feature that the children found especially difficult to match. Discuss ways in which the children can remember these features in future.

Differentiation
Younger or less able children can look at a smaller set of cards relating to a range of 2-D shapes and right angles. You could also use the cards to make hanging geometry mobiles with the names of the shapes on the back of the cards. Older and more able

AGE RANGE 9–11

LEARNING OBJECTIVE
To understand equivalent fractions.

CURRICULUM LINKS
KS2: MA2 2d, 2e.
NNS: Fractions and decimals (Y4–6, p22–25).

Fraction battleships

What you need
Squared paper cut into 10 by 10 grids, pencils; plain paper.

What to do
● Organise the children into pairs and give each player a pencil and two 10 by 10 grids. Tell the children that they are going to play a version of battleships.
● Before starting the game, give the children a few fractions to find on their grids. For example, challenge them to find the target squares for $\frac{2}{10}$, $\frac{4}{5}$ and $\frac{30}{100}$, $\frac{70}{100}$ (2 across, 8 down, and 3 across, 7 down).
● Explain that they can reduce a fraction to an equivalent fraction by dividing both numerator and denominator by the same number. For example, $\frac{2}{10}$ is the same as $\frac{1}{5}$.
● Invite the players to mark their fleet on one of their grids using crosses. Each vessel covers a different number of squares and they should have a total of ten vessels on their grid:
    One battleship covering four squares
    Two cruisers, each covering three squares
    Three destroyers, each covering two squares
    Four submarines, each covering one square.
● The vessels may only be positioned vertically or horizontally, not diagonally.
● When each player has marked their fleet on their grid, it's time to play.
● In turn, the players call out co-ordinates in equivalent fractions to make a shot at their partner's fleet. The other player must work out the fraction co-ordinates and say whether the shot has missed or hit and what it has hit. If a player hits a target successfully they may have another go.
● The players should use their spare grid to mark the spots where they have hit their partner's ships.
● The winner is the first player to hit all of their partner's fleet.
● After the game, encourage the children to make different sized grids, such as 8 by 8, and investigate other types of equivalent fractions

Differentiation
Play a whole-class game with younger children, using simple fractions. For example, a 10 by 10 grid would have co-ordinates of $\frac{3}{10}$, $\frac{6}{10}$. Draw a fleet on a grid and then play the group game on a large blank grid drawn on the board. More able children could find the fractions and then convert them into the equivalent decimals.

Robot by numbers

Dice total	Robot design
3	Left Leg
4	Right Leg
5	Head
6	Top part of body
7	Lower part of body
8	Left arm
9	Right arm
10	Left foot
11	Right foot
12	Eye
13	Eye
14	Ear
15	Ear
16	Right hand
17	Left hand
18	Mouth

PHOTOCOPIABLE

SCHOLASTIC

Fraction pizzas 1

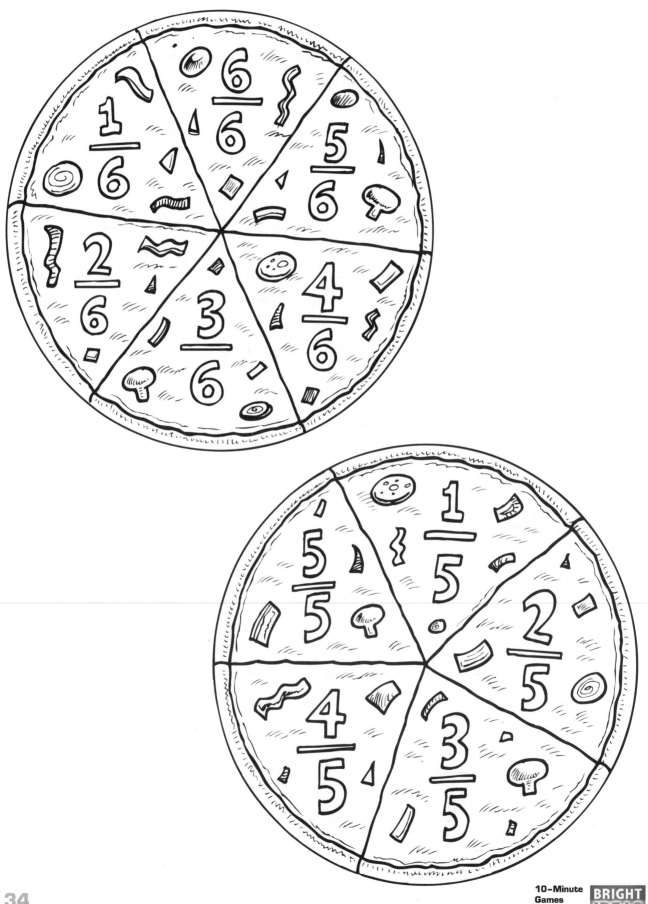

10–Minute Games

BRIGHT IDEAS

Fraction pizzas 2

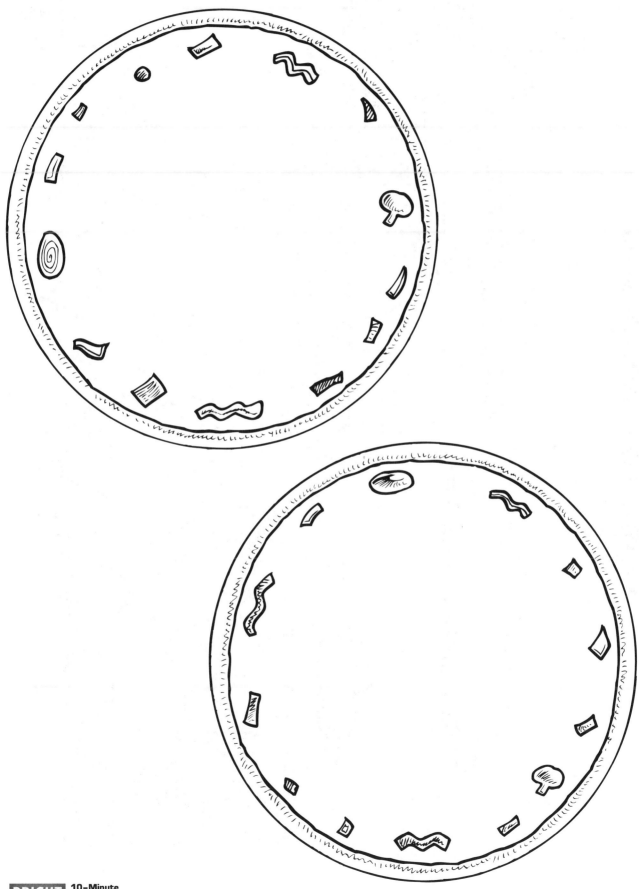

Climb the Mountains

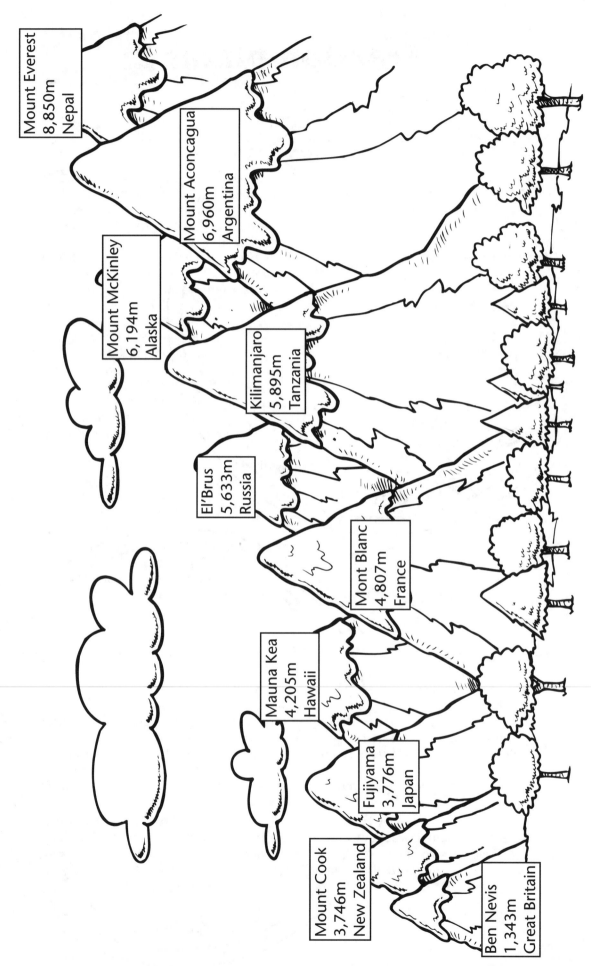

Mount Everest
8,850m
Nepal

Mount Aconcagua
6,960m
Argentina

Mount McKinley
6,194m
Alaska

Kilimanjaro
5,895m
Tanzania

El'Brus
5,633m
Russia

Mont Blanc
4,807m
France

Mauna Kea
4,205m
Hawaii

Fujiyama
3,776m
Japan

Mount Cook
3,746m
New Zealand

Ben Nevis
1,343m
Great Britain

10–Minute Games

BRIGHT IDEAS

PHOTOCOPIABLE

Geometry bingo
Picture cards

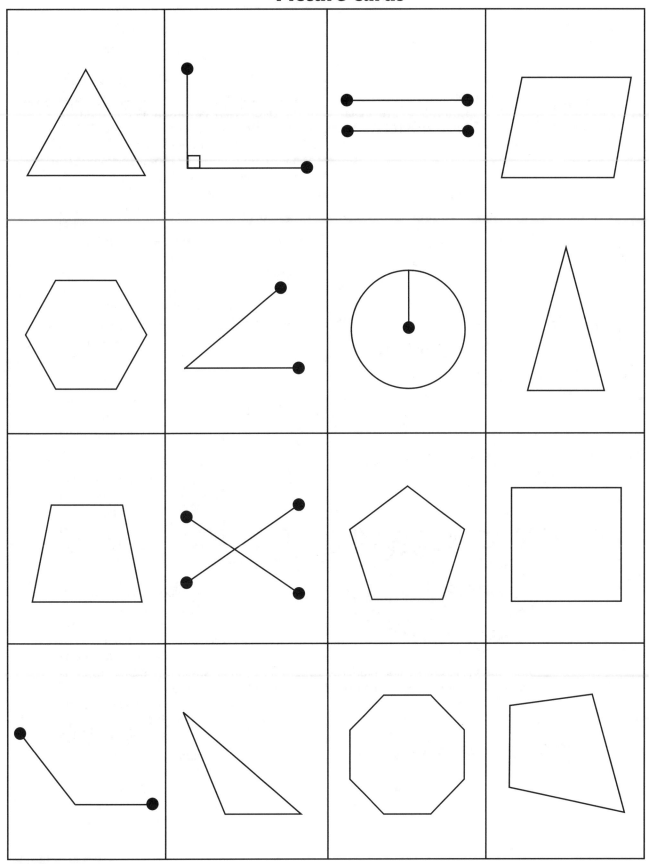

Geometry bingo
Word cards

equilateral triangle	right angle	parallel lines	parallelogram
hexagon	acute angle	radius	isosceles triangle
trapezium	intersecting lines	pentagon	square
obtuse angle	scalene triangle	octagon	quadrilateral

10-Minute Games **BRIGHT IDEAS**

CHAPTER 3

Science

AGE RANGE 5–7

LEARNING OBJECTIVE
To explore and describe the way everyday materials change when they are heated or cooled.

CURRICULUM LINKS
KS1: Sc3 2b. QCA Science: Unit 2d – Reversible and irreversible changes. NLS: Y2 T1 Text 17.

Material pairs

What you need
The 'Material pairs 1' and 'Material pairs 2' photocopiable sheets on pages 46 and 47 (one complete set of cards per group).

What to do
● Show the children some examples of the picture cards. Look at the picture card showing water being poured into an ice cube tray, and ask the children to predict what would happen if the tray of water was put in the freezer. When they have made their predictions, show them the ice cube card.
● Now show them the card showing a bar of chocolate. Ask the children to predict what would happen to the chocolate if it were heated up. Show them the card with a bowl of melted chocolate.
● Invite the children to play 'Material pairs'. Explain that they have to find pairs of cards that show the changes in different materials when they are heated or cooled.
● Organise the children into small groups of up to four. Shuffle each set of cards and spread them out, face down on the table.
● The first player should turn over a card and look at the picture, then turn over another card to see if the two pictures go together. For example, a correct pairing might be bread dough and a loaf of bread.
● If the cards go together, the player keeps them and has another turn.
● If the cards do not go together, the player must put them back in the exact places for the next player.
● The winner is the player with the most correct pairs of cards.
● At the end of the game invite the children to explain the changes of the materials from each set of their cards. Ask them which of the changes could be reversible. Can they think of any more materials that change when they are heated or cooled?

Differentiation
Younger children could use the cards to play a game using 'Snap' rules. Give each child a set of shuffled cards. If they see a matching liquid and solid pair of cards they should call out *Change*, and take all of the cards in the pile. Ask older and more able children to create their own cards to explore changes in, for example, materials that burn such as wood and coal.

AGE RANGE 5–7

LEARNING OBJECTIVE
To name and describe living things, materials, phenomena and processes.

CURRICULUM LINKS
KS1: Breadth of study 2a.

Scientific brainstorm!

What you need
A safe, open space.

What to do
● This game encourages children to think about names and terms in the different areas of science. It can fit in with your current or past science topics and could also be used for an initial brainstorming session or for consolidating information after an activity or lesson.

● Introduce a subject to the children, for example, green plants. Discuss briefly what the subject could cover. For example, the different parts of a flower, the names of different flowers or plants.

● Ask the children to stand in a circle and tell them that you are going to have a 'scientific brainstorm'. Explain that you will call out a subject, such as *Flowers*, and the children have to say quickly a word relating to the given subject.

● Call out the subject and point to a child to start the game. They have to quickly call out something related to the given subject, such as *stamen*.

● Going clockwise around the circle, challenge each child to call out a name or term related to flowers.

● If, on their turn, a child cannot think of any more words, they can call out *Pass*. At this point, call out another subject, such as *Minibeasts*, and continue playing.

● Keep playing until you have covered four or five different subject areas.

● At the end of the game, discuss some of the words that were mentioned. Write them on the whiteboard so that the children can see how many words they came up with. Together, think of some more words to add to the list.

Differentiation
Change the subject every third or fourth child with groups of younger or less able children. Encourage older or more able children to focus on just one scientific area. For example, words or terms related to *Light* could include *bright*, *dark*, *reflect*, *transparent* and *shadow*.

10–Minute Games

AGE RANGE 5–9

LEARNING OBJECTIVE
To understand that pushing is an example of a force.

CURRICULUM LINKS
KS1 and KS2: Sc4 2b.
QCA Science: Unit 1e – Pushes and pulls; Unit 2e – Forces and movement.

Bubble competition

What you need
Bowls of bubble mixture (ten parts warm water to one part concentrated washing-up liquid); empty, clean plastic washing-up liquid bottles with the bottoms cut off (this game is best played out in the playground!).

What to do

● Explain to the children that they are going to play a game to make bubble shapes. Ask them to show you the different ways that they can blow through their mouths. For example, blowing gently and then hard, or blowing in long, drawn-out breaths and then short, sharp bursts.
● Ask the children to guess what kind of bubble could be made from a long, gentle blow.
● Put the large end of a cut-off washing-up liquid bottle in the soapy water then do a long gentle blow through the lid end. Was the children's hypothesis correct?
● Arrange the children into teams of three and explain that they have to find a blowing technique that will produce the biggest bubble in the class.
● The bubbles must float away from the end of the containers in order to be judged.
● Each team has three chances (one per child) and they have just three minutes to experiment and practise blowing bubbles.
● Remind the children that it is very important that they blow and not suck, and that teams will be disqualified if they mess about with the bubble mixture.
● Distribute the containers and bubble mixture among the teams. After three minutes, ask everyone to stop, then invite each team in turn to show their efforts to the rest of the group.
● Award one point for each bubble that floats away from the end of the container, and two points for each big bubble.
● Count up the points to find the winning team
● At the end of the competition, ask the children who made the biggest bubbles to compete against each other to find the bubble-blowing champion.
● Ask the winning team or child to describe the technique that they used to blow their biggest bubble.

Differentiation
Provide younger children with a range of bubble-blowing devices and let them have fun making lots of bubbles using different techniques. Give older and more able children large hoops made from wire or plastic and encourage them to try to make different-shaped bubbles.

Materials charades

AGE RANGE 7–8

LEARNING OBJECTIVE
To understand that materials are suitable for making a particular object because of their properties and that some properties are more important than others when deciding what to use.

CURRICULUM LINKS
KS2: Sc3 1a.
QCA Science: 3c – Characteristics of materials.

What you need

A safe, open space; objects made from one material such as a plastic bottle, wooden ruler, paper book, glass jar, metal spoon and cotton top; objects made from a mix of materials such as a plastic chair with metal legs or a woollen jumper with a metal zip.

What to do

● Show the children the objects made from just one material. As you hold up each object in turn, ask the children what is it made from.
● Now do the same with the objects made from a mix of materials. Notice that many objects are made from more than one material.
● Organise the children into pairs. Invite them to play a game of 'Material charades'.
● Explain to the children that, in their pairs, they have to choose an object and decide which material or materials it is made from. They must then mime a situation in which the object is used. Before starting start their mime, the pair can say if the object is made from one type of material or a mix.
● The other pairs have to guess what the object is and the material or materials that it is made from.
● The chosen pair have just two minutes to make up the mime to show to the rest of the class.
● Invite one pair to start. Give one point to the first pair to guess the mime correctly.
● When all of the mimes have been guessed, talk about the different materials and uses that the children mimed. Challenge the children to think about why some particular materials are used for certain objects such as paper towels, or plastic bottles.

Differentiation

Play a simpler game with younger children. Organise them into five groups, each named after a material such as *glass, wood, metal, cloth* and *plastic*. Make up a sentence and when the children hear you mention an object made that is from their material, they must run to the end of the hall and then back to their places again. Older or more able children could use the mime game to highlight the different properties of materials, such as strength, flexibility and magnetic behaviour. Encourage them to think up charade signs to indicate these properties at the beginning of the game.

AGE RANGE 7–11

LEARNING OBJECTIVE
To be aware of the importance of an adequate and varied diet for health.

CURRICULUM LINKS
KS2: Sc2 2b.
QCA Science: 3a – Teeth and eating; 5a – Keeping healthy.

The balance of good health

What you need
A safe, open space; 'The balance of good health' photocopiable sheet on page 48; five A4 cards with one food group written on each (starches/carbohydrates, fruit/vegetables, milk/dairy, fats/sugars, proteins); small cards, each with the name of a different type of food and drink (one per child).

What to do
● Begin by talking about the different food groups that make up a healthy balanced diet.
● Mark out a 'Balance of health' plate on the ground using chalk or a length of rope and divide the circle to represent each section. Place the food group name cards in the appropriate sections and ask the children to read the names.
● Check that the children understand which types of foods go in each section by asking them to name, for example, five foods that would go into the 'proteins' section. Can anyone suggest why the fats/sugars section is smaller than the fruit/vegetable section?
● Tell the children that you have written cards with the name of a food such as pasta, lentils, nuts, chocolate and tuna, and give one card to each child.
● Ask the children to stand in a line, at least five metres from the big plate.
● When you give the instruction, the children have to run to the plate and stand in the correct section for the card that they are holding.
● Check each child in turn to see if they are standing in the correct section. If anyone is in the wrong section, ask the group to suggest where they should be standing.
● At the end of the game ask the children to swap the cards among themselves and go back to the starting line, then start the game again.
● At the end of the game, discuss the importance of a balanced diet. Help the children to understand that some food groups should be taken in smaller quantities than others.
● **Note:** In a balanced diet, the food groups are divided as: starches/carbohydrates 33%; fruit/vegetables 33%; milk/dairy 15%; fats/sugars 8%; proteins 12%.

Differentiation
Give younger or less able children small picture cards rather than word cards. Write or draw examples of the food in the different sections of the balance of good health plate, and encourage the children to run and stand by the drawings that match their cards. Challenge older and more able children to make their own word and picture cards with additional examples from each section of the plates.

The food chain race

AGE RANGE 7–11

LEARNING OBJECTIVE
To see how food chains show feeding relationships in a habitat.

CURRICULUM LINKS
KS2: Sc2 5d, 5e.
QCA Science: Unit 4b – Habitats; Unit 6a – Interdependence and adaptation.

What you need
A safe, open space; the 'Food chain race' photocopiable sheet on page 49 (cut into individual cards, ensuring that you have one card per child).

What to do
● The aim of this game is for the children to find out which food chain they are in and in what order they belong.
● Begin by talking about food chains with the children. Emphasise that nearly all food chains start with a green plant.
● Ask the children to give you an example of a four-link food chain. For example, pond plants are eaten by pond insects, which are eaten by fish, which are eaten by humans.
● Give each child a card from the photocopiable sheet. Explain that each of the living things on the cards forms part of a four-link food chain, and that each food chain comes from a different habitat such as a pond, ocean, African plains or a British wood.
● On the word *Go*, challenge the children to find the other three children who are part of their food chain.
● Once they have found each other, the food chain groups must put themselves into the correct food chain order.
● The winner is the first group in the correct order in a complete food chain.
● At the end of the game, use the winning team to highlight the 'producer', 'primary consumer', 'secondary consumer' and 'tertiary consumer' in the food chain.
● Redistribute the cards to different children and play the game again.

Differentiation
Show younger or less able children pictures of three-link food chains before starting the game, then lay out these food chain pictures on the floor in different parts of the room. Give each child a picture card or name of one thing from a food chain and invite them to find their correct food chain in the room. Challenge more able children to find their food chain team by asking each other questions. For example, *Do you live in water?* or *Are you a carnivore?*.

AGE RANGE 7–11

LEARNING OBJECTIVE
To understand that objects are pulled downwards because of the gravitational attraction between them and the Earth.

CURRICULUM LINKS
KS2: Sc4 2b.
QCA Science: 6e – Forces in action.

Keep the balloons up!

What you need
A safe, open indoor space; balloons (more than one per child in case of accidents!); a net or rope.

What to do
● Show the children a blown-up balloon. Can anyone suggest why it is light? (Because it is full of air.)
● Throw the balloon up into the air and then let it float down to the ground. Ask the children why the balloon didn't stay in the air even though it was light. Briefly discuss how the gravitational pull of the Earth brought the balloon down.
● Organise the children into two teams with eight players in each team.
● Divide the indoor area down the middle with a net or a rope on the floor and ask the teams to face each other on opposite sides of the net or rope.
● Give each team member a balloon. On the word *Go*, the teams should hit their balloons over to the opposing team's section.
● They can use any part of their bodies to do this, such as their heads, legs, arms and feet.
● The challenge of the game is to keep the balloons from touching the floor within their half of the hall.
● If any balloon hits the ground within either team's section, the game is stopped and the opposing team get a point.
● Make sure that everyone has a balloon, then start the game again.
● After three minutes, change the teams so that everyone has a chance to play.
● At the end of the game, ask the children if they found it easy keeping the balloons up in the air. Can they suggest another object to use that would make the game more difficult? Discuss why heavier objects would make the game more difficult (stronger gravitational pull).

Differentiation
Organise younger or less able children into small teams and, standing in circles, challenge them to see which team can keep their balloon up in the air the longest. To make the game more of a challenge for older or more able children, replace the balloons with footballs or netballs. Give each team four balls and compare the results with the balloon game.

■SCHOLASTIC

Material pairs 1

■SCHOLASTIC

PHOTOCOPIABLE

Material pairs 2

The balance of good health

PHOTOCOPIABLE

Mini pictures 1

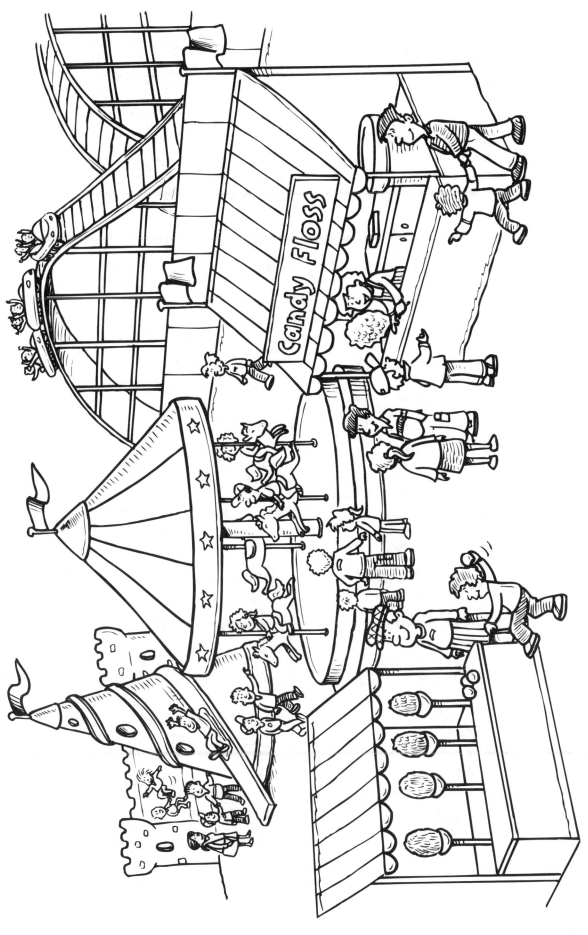

◖SCHOLASTIC

Mini pictures 2

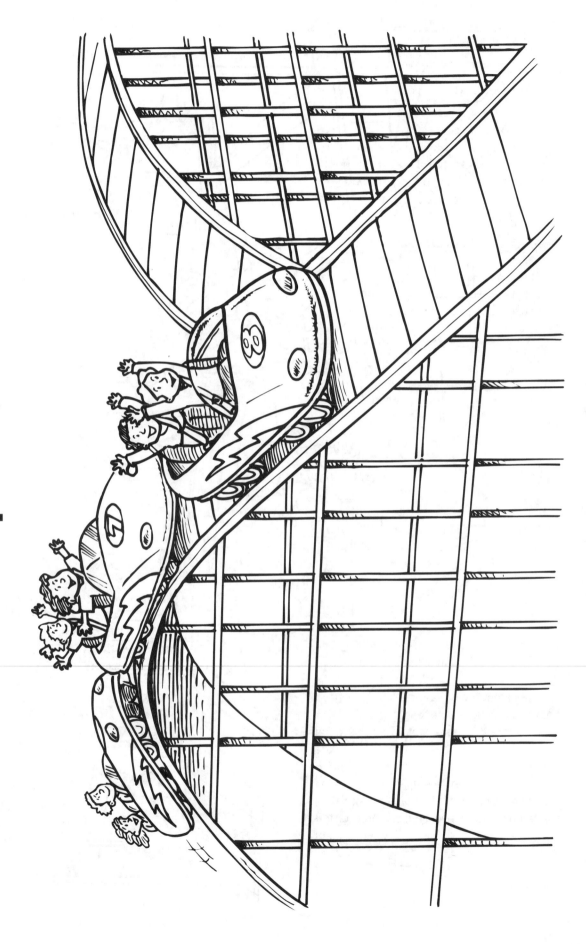

AGE RANGE 5–7

LEARNING OBJECTIVE
To listen and recognise different pulses and rhythms.

CURRICULUM LINKS
KS1: 2b, 4a, 4c.
QCA Music: Unit 4 – Feel the pulse.

Musical instructions

What you need
A tambourine or drum; beanbags.

What to do
● Ask the children to sit in a large circle. Start beating the drum or tambourine in steady beats. Encourage the children to copy the beat by patting their laps.
● Change the beat to give different tempos such as slow, walking speed, fast, and very fast. Ask the children for some more examples of tempo such as galloping or trotting speeds. Each time you change, encourage the children to copy you.
● Try different dynamics with the beat, such as very quiet and very loud. Briefly look at more examples of dynamics, such as moving from very quiet to quiet, or from loud to very loud.
● Now explain to the children that they are going to have to concentrate even harder because you are going to give them a beanbag to pass round in time to the beat.
● Explain that as the beanbag goes around the circle, the children have to listen for different sound instructions for the beanbag. The child who has the beanbag when a sound instruction is made has to follow the instruction correctly, while the rest of the group keep the beat going.
● Choose instructions to match your children's abilities, for example:

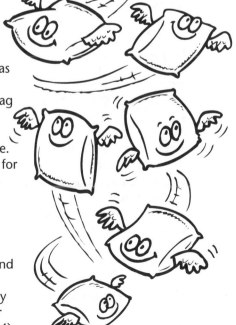

> One loud beat means that the beanbag has to be thrown in the air
> Four quick beats means change the direction of the beanbag
> Shaking the tambourine means that the beanbag has to thrown to another child in the circle
> Six galloping beats means the child with the beanbag has to get up and skip around the circle.

● Run through the instructions with the children until they are familiar with them then enjoy playing the game.
● Encourage the children to think of more instructions for the game next time they play.

Differentiation
Let younger children break off from the beat while the child holding the beanbag does the appropriate action. Older or more able children could use two bean bags and set them off in opposite directions. It can be interesting if a child gets both bean bags at once. Vary the game by using different types of instruments such as a chime bar or recorder. Try out different beats such as two time (2/4), three time (3/4) or galloping in a 6/4 time.

AGE RANGE 7–11

LEARNING OBJECTIVE
To recognise rhythmic patterns through listening and to recognise musical notation.

CURRICULUM LINKS
KS2: 4a, 4c.
QCA Music: Unit 10 – Play it again.

Musical hoops

What you need
The 'Musical hoops' photocopiable sheet on page 79 (you will need two complete, enlarged sets of the rhythm cards); 16 PE hoops; a safe, open area; a drum.

What to do
● The photocopiable sheet shows two identical sets of rhythm patterns. Using just one set of patterns from one of the sheets, hold up each of the eight cards in turn and invite the children to clap out the rhythm on each card with you. Repeat several times, so that the children are happy with the pattern of each of the rhythms.

● Set out the hoops around the open space in a random pattern, leaving enough space around the outside of the hoops for the children to move freely and safely.

● Using a complete set of 16 rhythm cards, place one card in the middle of each hoop. Keep the other complete set for yourself.

● Ask the children to dance around the hoops to a simple beat of your drum. When you stop playing they must freeze on the spot.

● Beat out one of the

rhythmic phrases from the cards. When you have finished say, *Where is my rhythm?*.
● The children have to run around the room until they find a hoop that contains the rhythm card that matches your pattern.
● When everyone is in a hoop, walk around the room to see if they are correct. Any children who are in the wrong hoops must go and sit at the side.
● Continue with the game, playing different rhythmic patterns from the cards.
● The winner is the last child in the game.

Differentiation
Use just four different, simple beats for younger or less able children. Challenge older children to have a go at playing the beat for the rest of the group to guess.

AGE RANGE 7–11

LEARNING OBJECTIVE
To listen to a piece of music and continue its tune and rhythm once it has stopped.

CURRICULUM LINKS
KS2: 1a, 2a, 4a.
QCA Music: Unit 16 – Cyclic patterns.

Karaoke challenge

What you need
A well-known piece of music such as Prokofiev's *Peter and the Wolf* or Gershwin's *Rhapsody in Blue*; pop or jazz music; a tape recorder or CD player.

What to do
● Explain to the children that most types of music have a distinct beat and tune. Choose an example of a well-known piece of music and ask the children to listen carefully to the beat and the main tune. Encourage the children to join in and establish the musical beat by clapping the beat and humming along with the main tune.
● Tell the children that at some point you will turn down the music, but you would like them to continue with the tune and beat. Turn down the volume for 30 seconds and then turn it up again so that the children can hear whether they have kept to the beat and tune.
● Organise the children into groups of three or four. Challenge to groups to listen to some more music and keep the beat and tune going once it has been turned down.
● Choose a group to start, and play them a piece of music. Without warning, turn the music down so that the group cannot hear it. Challenge them to continue the beat and tune of the music. After a brief period, turn up the music to see how close the group have kept to the original beat and tune.
● Use different music or different parts of the same piece of music for each group.
● When each group has had a turn, decide who the winners should be by discussing which team did the best at keeping to the original tune and beat.
● If two groups came very close, play more music at longer intervals until you have established a winner.

Differentiation
Choose simple songs such as *Head, shoulders, knees and toes* for younger children. Sing the song through and clap the beats together, then cut out different phrases each time the song is repeated. Encourage older or more able children to improvise the tune over the regular beat of the piece of music. When you turn up the music, check to see if they have kept up with the original beat.

AGE RANGE 7–11

LEARNING OBJECTIVE
To understand how sounds can be used to illustrate stories.

CURRICULUM LINKS
KS1 1c, 2b, 3a, 4b.
QCA Music: Unit 6 – What's the score?

Sound charades

What you need
Instruments such as drums, triangles, chime bars, tambourines, shakers, kazoos; titles of well-known fairy tales such as *Cinderella*, *Jack and the Beanstalk* and *The Three Billy Goats Gruff* written on pieces of paper; paper; pens.

What to do
● Organise the children into groups of four. Give each group a pen and a piece of paper. Place the instruments on a table at the other side of the room.
● Explain that the children are going to play a game. They have one minute in which to use the instruments to illustrate a well-known fairy story. The rest of the children will listen to the sounds and try to guess the story.
● Tell them that they must not speak, hum or make any sound with their voices, but they can use mime to perform their story. They can only use their instruments to make sounds.
● Discuss how they can use the instruments to illustrate characters, moods and settings through tempo, dynamics, duration, pitch, timbre or combining sounds together.
● Choose one group to come up and take a piece of paper. The children must go over to the instrument table and choose the instruments that they need to mime their fairy tale.
● Give them one minute to think about their sound charade, then invite them to perform their musical mime to the other groups.
● At the end of the charade, ask the rest of the children to write down the name of the story that they think the group was miming.
● Ask each group to read out their answers, then ask the performing group for the correct answer.
● Award a point to each team with the correct answer, then invite another group to take a turn.
● When each group has performed their sound charade, count up the points to find the winning team.

Differentiation
Ask younger children to use the instruments to depict certain types of moods or weather. Encourage them to think about the dynamics, tempo, timbre and the duration of the sounds that they are making. Older or more able children could mime well-known stories, myths or legends from other cultures, using their instruments in the style of that culture, such as Indian sounds for an Indian folk tale.

10–Minute Games

AGE RANGE 7–11

LEARNING OBJECTIVE
To match a beat pattern with the correct note lengths.

CURRICULUM LINKS
KS2: 4c.
QCA Music: Units 8 and 15 – ongoing skills.

Match the notes

What you need
The 'Match the notes 1' and 'Match the notes 2' photocopiable sheets on pages 80 and 81. (You will need one gameboard per child and two sets of note length cards per pair of children.)

What to do
● Tell the children that they are going to play a game in pairs. Begin by discussing how musical notes represent lengths of different beats. Look at the note list from the 'Match the note 2' photocopiable sheet, and talk about the note signs and their respective beat lengths:

> a quaver = half a beat
> crotchet = one beat
> minim = two beats
> semibreve = four beats.

● Ask the children to count and clap out the beat lengths.
● Explain that the note signs can go together to make rhythmic phrases. Using the game board, show the children an example of a three-beat note pattern. Ask them to name each note in the pattern and its length. Now ask them to clap out the note pattern.
● Organise the children into pairs and give each child a copy of the game board and note list. Shuffle together two sets of note length cards and put them face down between the two players.
● In turn, each player should turn over a card. If the note lengths on the card match the number of beats in a square on the game board, the player can place that card on the appropriate square.
● If the player cannot find a matching square, they must put the card to one side and let the next player take a turn.
● Once the players have worked through the pile of note cards, they must shuffle the remaining cards and try again.
● The winner is the first player to cover all of their squares with the correct notes.

Differentiation
Use the game boards to play bingo with younger children. Look at a card and clap out the note rhythm. The children have to count the beats and cover the correct number with a counter or piece of paper. The first child to cover up their board is the winner. Older or more able children can make up their note length patterns and challenge other child or group to match them on the board. Encourage them to make their own game boards using a couple of bars of note patterns.

AGE RANGE 7–11

LEARNING OBJECTIVE
To sing a song using a range of musical styles and elements.

CURRICULUM LINKS
KS2: 1a, 1c, 2a, 4b.
QCA Music: Unit 11 – The class orchestra.

Change that tune!

What you need
Knowledge of familiar tunes and songs such as pop songs or assembly songs; timer or stop watch.

What to do
● Organise the children into groups of three or four. Give each group a well-known song to sing.
● Tell the children that you would like them to imagine that they are making a record in a recording studio. You are the record producer and will call out instructions to them while they are singing. Explain that they must immediately follow your instructions.
● Ask one group to begin singing. After a short time, give an instruction to the group, for example:

Change the style of music and sing it in a operatic style, rap style, country and western style or a lullaby style
Change the tempo to go faster or slower
Change the volume to make it louder or quieter
Change the rhythm
Change the timbre
Change the mood

● You could also ask the other groups for other suggestions for instructions.
● Call out the instructions to challenge their concentration. You could call out a couple of instructions within a few seconds or leave them in anticipation for a short while.
● If the children lose their concentration or start to laugh, they should stop and let the next group have a go.
● Time the groups so that you can see which group lasts the longest without losing concentration.
● If two groups last for the same length of time, give them a new song as a play off.

Differentiation
Younger or less able children could sing simple nursery rhymes as a group or class as you call out simple instructions. Stop the game if anyone starts giggling or loses track, then start the game again with another nursery rhyme. Challenge older or more able children to take turns to call out the instructions. Encourage them to use the correct musical language and make their instructions clear. For more of a challenge, instruct a group to change to another tune halfway through.

Musical hoops

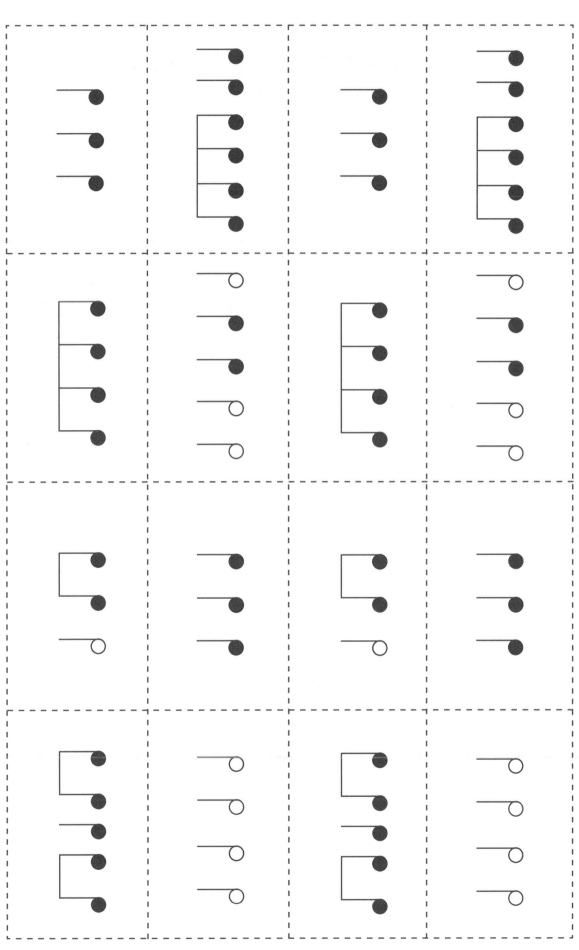

📖 S C H O L A S T I C

Match the notes 1

2 beats	6 beats	4 beats
4 beats	3 beats	2 beats
3 beats	4 beats	1 beat

6 beats	4 beats	2 beats
3 beats	2 beats	6 beats
3 beats	4 beats	3 beats

Match the notes 2

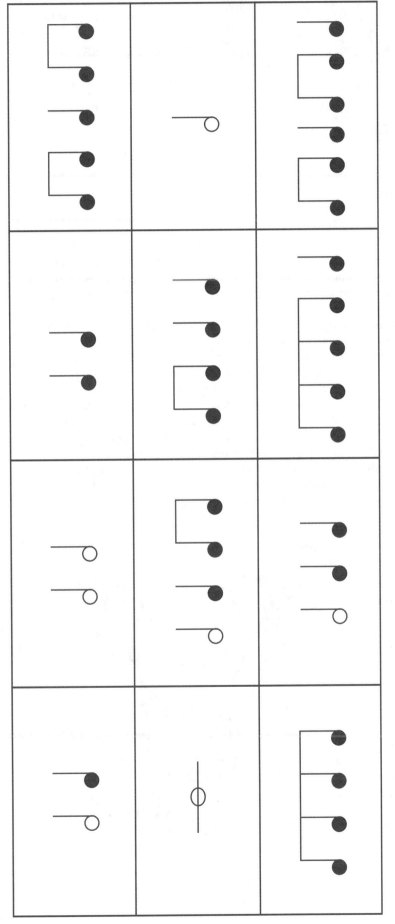

Note list

Name of note	Note sign	Length of note
A quaver		½ beat
A crotchet		1 beat
A minim		2 beats
A semi-breve		4 beats

CHAPTER 7

Physical education

AGE RANGE 5–7

LEARNING OBJECTIVE
To get into an area quickly before a time limit is up; to listen to instructions and work out a strategy to stay in the game.

CURRICULUM LINKS
KS1: 1a, 1b.

Corners

What you need
A safe, open area.

What to do
● Begin by talking about the importance of listening to instructions and performing them quickly and correctly during a game. Encourage the children to give examples of games or physical activities where instructions are important such as football, hockey, netball, dance and gymnastics

● Invite the children to play a game called 'Corners'. Give each corner of the room a colour, such as red, green, yellow and blue.

● Explain to the children that, when you say the word *Corners*, they have to run to any of the four corners in the room. You will choose a corner and all those children in that corner are out. The aim is to be the last player in the game.

● Go to one side of the room and turn your back to the children. Call out *Corners*, then let the children run to their chosen corners. Still with your back to the children, say, for example, *I choose the red corner*, then turn around quickly. Any child who has not reached a corner is out, and all of the children in the chosen corner are also out.

● Choose a child who is out to take your place and let him or her call out the instructions. Make sure their back is turned when they choose a coloured corner.

● Repeat the game until one child is left. That child is the winner of the game.

● After the game, ask the children what tactics they used in order to stay in the game.

Differentiation
Give younger children plenty of time to run to their chosen corner, so that there is less chance of them being out. Extend the game to incorporate specific skills for older children. Instead of colours, allocate a games, dance or gymnastic skill to each corner. When you turn around, the children must all be doing the set activity. If a child is not doing the activity, they are out, along with the chosen corner group.

Gymnastic sequences

AGE RANGE 5–7

LEARNING OBJECTIVE
To remember, repeat and link combinations of gymnastic actions, body shapes and balances with control and precision.

CURRICULUM LINKS
KS1: 8b, 8c.

What you need
A safe, open space.

What to do
● This game can be played as a class, or in groups. If you are playing it as a group game, organise the children into groups of five or six.
● Begin by talking about gymnastic performances. Discuss the skill of the gymnasts in linking different actions to make a sequence. Talk about ways in which one gymnastic action can lead naturally on to another, such as a forward roll followed by a star jump.
● Explain that the children are going to play a game to build up a sequence of gymnastic actions by remembering the previous actions of the other children and adding another action on to the end.
● Invite each child to think of one short gymnastic action. Offer examples, such as forward rolls, star jumps or hops. Encourage the children to think about different movements such as turning and rolling, balancing, taking off and landing, direction and speed, use of arms and legs.
● Number the groups then ask them to find a space in the room and stand together in a circle. Choose one child in the circle to perform their action. The next child should copy that action and then perform their own action.
● Keep going around their circle, with each child adding new actions to the previous sequence. Challenge the children to see how long they can continue and build on the sequence.
● If any child forgets an action, or performs it incorrectly, they are out. The winner is the last child left in the circle.
● Invite the winners to perform the entire sequence to the rest of the class.

Differentiation
Work with up to three younger children at a time and allocate actions for them to perform. Older children could play the game in groups of teams. Encourage them to perform a short sequence, which is then copied and added to by the next group. Encourage a sense of competition between groups by asking them to think of ways that they can vary their sequence, making it harder for other groups to remember all the actions.

AGE RANGE 5–7

LEARNING OBJECTIVE
To pass and throw a ball to hit a skittle using tactics in attacking and defending; to develop skills in dodging and shadowing an opponent.

CURRICULUM LINKS
KS1: 7a, 7b.

Hit the skittle

What you need
Two skittles; small ball; safe, open area; tabards or sashes in two different colours.

What to do
● Begin by demonstrating the skills needed to shadow or dodge an opponent. Tell the children that they are going to play a game, and they will need to keep alert and look for spaces to avoid their opponent when passing and receiving the ball.
● Choose two children: one defender and one attacker. Encourage the attacker to dodge the defender to find a space, and the defender to shadow the attacker closely.
● Stand two skittles in the centre of the play area, approximately ten metres away from each other. Organise the children into two teams, A and B, and invite them to put on the tabards to show which team they are in. Assign a skittle to each team.
● Explain that the aim of the game is to knock over the other team's skittle with a ball.
● Choose one child from each team to guard his or her team's skittle and organise the other children into pairs; one from Team A and one from Team B. Ask everyone to find a space in the hall or play area.
● To start the game, throw the ball into the air. Whoever catches it must try to pass it to another child in their team, without their partner getting it first.
● If a child has the ball they must not move until they have thrown it.
● The ball must be thrown, not hit, except by the skittle guard who can hit the ball away, but not kick it.
● Stress that nobody, except the skittle guard, should be within five or six feet of the skittle. This will help them to develop their throwing and aiming skills.
● The winners are the first team to knock down their opponent's skittle.

Differentiation
Younger children could use a beanbag and try to hit a larger target, such as a PE hoop.
For more able children, use two small balls and allocate two guards to each skittle.

AGE RANGE 5–11

LEARNING OBJECTIVES
To throw and aim with precision at a small area; to stay alert and defend an area from an oncoming ball.

CURRICULUM LINKS
KS1: 2, 7a, 7b.

Through the legs

What you need
Three or four balls; large, open area.

What to do
● Safety: remind the children that they must not kick the balls or throw them overarm in this game.
● Organise the children into teams of three or four and number each team.
● Ask each child in Team One to get a ball, and the other children to stand in a big circle with their legs apart and their feet touching the children on either side of them.
● Explain the rules: Team One will begin in the middle of the circle, and they need to think of ways in which they can outwit the defenders in order to get their balls out of the circle. The children in the circle have to be alert and try to stop the balls.
● Invite Team One to take up position in the middle of the circle. On the word *Go*, they have to try to throw their balls underarm through the legs of the other children. Every time they get a ball through, they score a goal.
● The children making the circle must not move but they may use their hands to stop the balls.
● Each team has one minute in the middle to try to score their goals. Once the minute is up, the next team goes into the middle and the previous team joins the circle.
● The team with the most goals are the winners.

Differentiation
Younger children could play the game in smaller circles with just one child and one ball in the middle. Older children could play a variation of the game to practise throwing and defending skills. Put the children into two teams. One team makes an inner circle and the other team stands behind them in an outer circle. Two or three members of the outer circle team go into the middle and try to throw balls to their team mates while the inner circle team try to hit the balls out of the way.

AGE RANGE 5–11

LEARNING OBJECTIVE
To throw and catch a ball with accuracy and speed; to be aware of another group's different activity.

CURRICULUM LINKS
KS1: 7a.
KS2: 7c.

Who is faster?

What you need
A safe, open space; two benches; a ball.

What to do
● Invite the children to play a game. Explain that they are going to be organised into two teams, each performing a different activity. One team will be throwing and catching while the other team runs around a set course. The aim of the game is to see how many catches one team can achieve in the time that it takes the other team to run around the course. Each team will know how the other team is doing by listening to the number of catches or team numbers being called out.
● Place the benches in opposite corners of the room, leaving enough space for the children to run around them.
● Organise the children into Team A and Team B.
● For the catching activity, Team A should form a circle in the middle of the room. One player stands in the centre holding a ball. On the word *Go*, that player throws the ball to a player in the circle who throws it back. This counts as one catch and the team calls out *One*, then the player throws the ball to the next child in the circle. Every time there is a catch, the team calls out the number. If the ball is dropped they have to start counting from one again.
● For the running activity, number each of the players in Team B and ask them to line up about two metres behind one of the benches. On the word *Go*, the player at the front of the line calls out their number and runs around the outside of the benches before joining the end of the line. The next player then calls out their number and runs around the benches, and so on.
● When everyone in Team B has completed their circuit, call out *Stop*.
● Ask Team A to tell you the total number of catches, which is their overall score.
● Swap the teams over and repeat the activity. The team with the highest score at the end of the game is the winner.

Differentiation
Work with teams of up to four younger children. Make the game more competitive for older children by having a set amount of catches for Team A to achieve. Challenge Team B by adding obstacles to the running course.

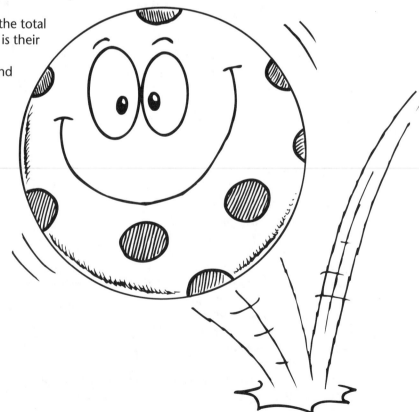

AGE RANGE 7–11

LEARNING OBJECTIVE
To practice striking skills by using small balls to hit a larger target.

CURRICULUM LINKS
KS2: 1b, 7b, 7c.

Move the football

What you need
Two skittles; small ball; safe, open area; tabards or sashes in two different colours.

What to do
● Begin by demonstrating the skills needed to shadow or dodge an opponent. Tell the children that they are going to play a game, and they will need to keep alert and look for spaces to avoid their opponent when passing and receiving the ball.

● Choose two children: one defender and one attacker. Encourage the attacker to dodge the defender to find a space and the defender to shadow the attacker closely.

● Stand two skittles in the centre of the play area, approximately ten metres away from each other. Organise the children into two teams, A and B, and invite them to put on the tabards to show which team they are in. Assign a skittle to each team.

● Explain that the aim of the game is to knock over the other team's skittle with a ball.

● Choose one child from each team to guard his or her team's skittle and organise the

other children into pairs; one from Team A and one from Team B. Ask everyone to find a space in the hall or play area.

● To start the game, throw the ball into the air. Whoever catches it must try to pass it to another child in their team, without their partner getting it first.

● If a child has the ball they must not move until they have thrown it.

● The ball must be thrown, not hit, except by the skittle guard who can hit the ball away, but not kick it.

● Stress that nobody, except the skittle guard, should be within five or six feet of the skittle. This will help them to develop their throwing and aiming skills.

● The winners are the first team to knock down their opponent's skittle.

Differentiation
Younger or less able children could use a beanbag and try to hit a larger target, such as a PE hoop. For more able children, use two small balls and allocate two guards to each skittle.

AGE RANGE 7–11

LEARNING OBJECTIVE
To effectively field balls and pass them to team members; to throw balls that avoid or deceive the fielders in order to score runs.

CURRICULUM LINKS
KS2: 1b, 7a, 7b, 7c.

Throw ball

What you need
Hoop; two skittles; four small balls; a safe, open area.

What to do
● Prepare for the game by placing a big hoop on the ground with the four small balls inside it. Place one skittle by the hoop and put the other skittle at a distance that you think appropriate for the skills of your children.
● Organise the children into two teams, A and B.
● Explain that Team A will take turns to throw the balls and score runs, and Team B will be the fielders.
● Ask Team B to space themselves out across the play area, making sure that some are close to the hoop. Team A must stand back in a line.
● The first thrower from Team A goes into the hoop and throws out the four balls quickly, in any direction. The fielders in Team B have to return the balls to the hoop as quickly as possible. However, they cannot move with the ball, they can only pass or throw it. At least one fielder should be positioned next to the hoop so that he or she can place the ball in the hoop.
● When the thrower from Team A has thrown all the balls, he or she must run between the skittles until all four balls are back in the hoop and you call out *Stop*. Remind the thrower to keep score of the runs between the skittles.
● Once all of Team A have had a turn at throwing and running, ask them to change places with Team B.
● The winner is the team with the most runs.

Differentiation
Make sure younger children are within easy throwing and catching distance from each other. Challenge older children to return the balls to the hoop in a specified time limit.

CHAPTER 8

PSHE & citizenship

BRIGHT IDEAS

AGE RANGE 5–7

LEARNING OBJECTIVE
To understand that everyone belongs to various groups and communities, such as family and school.

CURRICULUM LINKS
KS1: 2f.
QCA Citizenship: Unit 5 – Living in a diverse world.

Totem communities

What you need
Large square sheets of paper; pencils or coloured pens; sticky tape.

What to do
● Tell the children that they are going to look at the different communities that are part of their everyday life. Discuss examples such as family, school, clubs, shops, places of worship and so on.

● Encourage the children to think of examples of things that happen in a school community. For example, a favourite lesson, playing with friends, having assembly or reading books.

● Explain that Native American Indians used totem poles to represent themselves or their family. The totem poles were divided into sections and illustrated different parts of their family or communities.

● Organise the children into groups of six and give each child a square piece of paper and a pencil.

● Introduce the game, explaining that each group is going to choose an example of a community and then draw a totem pole to represent it.

● On five pieces of paper, they should draw five examples of the community group they have chosen, and on the sixth sheet, they should draw an emblem to represent the community group. For a school, this could be a book and pen or the school emblem. Each child in the group has to draw just one of the sections.

● Ask each group to decide which community they would like to focus on, then give the children six minutes to think of their five examples and emblem and draw them on their paper.

● When the time limit is up, ask the children to tape the six drawings together to make their totem poles.

● Invite each group in turn to hold up their totem for the others to see. Challenge the rest of the class to guess the community and the different examples shown on the totem.

Differentiation
Provide a universal subject, such as school, for younger or less able children. Encourage them to work in pairs to make a large-scale totem that you can display in the entrance to your school. Older and more able children can make totems of different cultures and their beliefs, religious festivals and different geographical communities.

Faceless feelings

AGE RANGE 5–7

LEARNING OBJECTIVE
To recognise, name and deal with their feelings in a positive way.

CURRICULUM LINKS
KS1: 1c, 4a. 5b.
QCA Citizenship: Unit 1 – Taking part.

What you need

The 'Faceless feelings' photocopiable sheet on page 95 (copy on to card and cut out); scarf (optional); string or ribbon.

What to do

● Attach string or ribbon to the mask from the photocopiable sheet so that you can tie the mask on.
● Ask the children to sit in a circle. Encourage them to think of different feelings such as being scared, angry, happy, sad, excited and so on.
● Explain to the children that we tend to show our feeling through the expressions of our face. Ask the children to show a sad face. Help them to see that they mainly use their eyes and mouth to express sadness.
● Demonstrate how you can show a feeling without using your face. Put on the mask and shut your eyes, then use body movements to illustrate being sad.

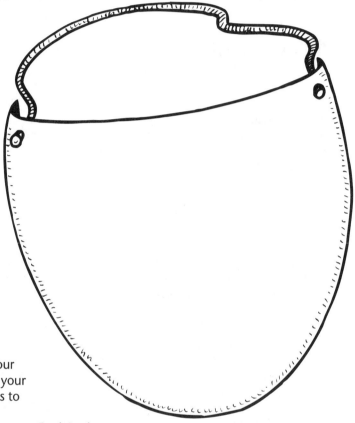

● Invite the children to play a game. Explain that they are going to think of a feeling, such as happiness, and a situation where they have that feeling, for example, opening a birthday present.
● Ask a child to come into the middle of the circle. Put the mask on them and ask them to close their eyes or gently tie the scarf over their eyes.
● Encourage them to convey a feeling and the situation to the class without speaking using just body movements and mime.
● Challenge the rest of the group to guess the feeling and the scenario. If a child guesses correctly, then it is their turn to go into the centre and mime.
● If no one gets the mime, ask the child to explain it, then choose another child to take a turn.
● It may be a good idea to have some ideas for feelings and scenarios for children who feel uncomfortable drawing on their own experiences. (Remember to remain sensitive when asking children about their experiences and feelings.)

Differentiation

Let younger children keep their eyes open throughout the mime. Older or more able children could use the game to look at situations where their actions affect themselves and others. For example, in pairs, they could wear masks to mime scenes about bullying, happiness due to an act of kindness or anger over an issue. Discuss the scenes and issues after each mime.

10–Minute Games

BRIGHT IDEAS

AGE RANGE 5–7

LEARNING OBJECTIVE
To identify and respect the differences and similarities between people.

CURRICULUM LINKS
KS1: 1a, 1b, 1d, 4b.4c, 5b, 5f.
QCA Citizenship: Unit 1 – Taking part; Unit 5 – Living in a diverse world.

Connections

What you need
A safe, open area.

What to do
● Begin by asking the children what they have in common with each other. Examples might include being in the same class, having two eyes and a nose. Next, ask the children about differences between them, such as different hairstyles, likes and dislikes or experiences.

● Explain that everyone can have a different view or idea of something. For example, ask the children to think of the first thing that comes into their mind when they hear the word *bread*. They may come up with ideas such as sandwiches, soup, flour, toast or packed lunch.

● Notice how an experience or word can trigger a connection to another experience or word. It could also make a connection to a feeling, for example: hot – ice cream.

● Tell the children that you are going to play a game. Explain that you are going to say one or two words to one of the children in the circle, for example, *bread*.

That child has to say the first thing that comes into their mind when they think about the given word or words, for example, *cheese sandwich*.

● The next child should say the first thing that comes into their head when they think of the previous child's word, for example, *picnic*.

● Each child in the circle must say their connections until a word gets back to you.

● It is fascinating to see where the connections can go. For example: bread – cheese sandwich – picnic – park – playing football – Man United – red – jumper – cold – winter.

● After the connections have gone round a full circle, discuss each one and why the children chose their connections.

● You will find the more the children play the game, the more sophisticated the connections become.

Differentiation
Play the game in smaller groups with less able children. Give them a set topic such as food, clothes or games and encourage them to see how many connections they can make in a set time. Older or more able children could look at connections about more complex areas including environmental issues, rules, people's jobs, spiritual, moral, social and cultural issues such as weddings and festivals.

Safety snapshots

AGE RANGE 7–11

LEARNING OBJECTIVE
To recognise the risks in different situations and then decide how to behave responsibly.

CURRICULUM LINKS
KS2: 3e, 3g, 5a, 5d.
QCA Citizenship: Unit 2 – Choices.

What you need
A safe, open space.

What to do
● Ask the children to name different situations where they could be at risk, such as the road, in the house, the park, by a river and so on.

● Choose one situation, such as a busy street, and ask the children to think of the possible dangers and risks that could occur, such as crossing between two cars, distracting drivers or running into the road to retrieve a ball.

● Introduce the game to the children by explaining that they are going to perform a one-minute sketch of an everyday scene, showing examples of possible dangers about to happen.

● Organise the children into six groups and give each group an everyday setting which they can relate to, such as a busy high street, a kitchen, the playground or the park.

● Explain that some of the children within the groups can play other parts, such as car drivers driving along the road.

● Discuss briefly how they could show different risks. For example, in the kitchen, a small child could be playing while an adult is cooking. The adult goes to answer the telephone, leaving the pan handle sticking out. Use clear mime or dialogue to show the events in the scene.

● Now tell the children that they have three minutes to think of a scene and practise it.

● After three minutes, ask everyone to sit on the floor and encourage each group in turn to show their scene.

● At the end of each scene, ask the other children what risks and danger were shown. Check with the performing group to see if the other children were correct.

● Follow up the game with an in-depth discussion about the different risks shown in the scenes and ways in which they can be avoided.

Differentiation
Younger and less able children could focus on one aspect of safety, such as road safety. Give each group a set scene and risk, such as a busy road and two children about to run out between two cars. Ask the others what they think is about to happen and what should happen. Adapt the game to help older children look at relationship issues such as bullying, and how children's actions can affect others and themselves.

Do you understand me?

AGE RANGE 7–11

LEARNING OBJECTIVE
To reflect on spiritual, moral, social and cultural issues, using empathy and imagination to understand other people's experiences.

CURRICULUM LINKS
KS2: 2e, 2i, 4a, 4f.
QCA Citizenship: Unit 1 – Taking part; Unit 2 – Choices; Unit 4 – People who help us; Unit 5 – Living in a diverse world.

What you need
Individual cards with sentences written on them (see below).

What to do
● Tell the children that they are going to play a game that will help them to understand what it must be like for someone who arrives in a different country and cannot speak the language. Discuss the experience of many people, especially immigrants, who arrive in a different country and find it difficult to communicate with others around them. Talk about how they must feel.

● Transcribe the following sentences on to pieces of card:

1 My bike has got a puncture.
2 Can I have a strawberry ice cream?
3 Have you seen my cat?
4 I think I have broken my arm.
5 Where is the post office?
6 Does the bus stop here?
7 I like your hairstyle.
8 Could you help me with these heavy boxes?
9 I like to go tap dancing.
10 Please do not smoke near me.

● Begin the game by asking a child to take a sentence card and read it silently. They have to try to get the meaning of the sentence over to the rest of the class without speaking.

● For example, using the sentence, *I've missed my bus*, the child could imitate the sound of the bus coming, then run on the spot to show that they are running after the bus. Finally they could use their face and hands to show that they missed the bus.

● Challenge the other children to guess the meaning of the sentence. They do not have to get the words exactly right but it is important that they get the meaning. For example, *I have broken my arm* could also be *I have hurt my arm very badly*, but *I have hurt my arm* is not precise enough.

● After the mime, give the children up to 30 seconds to guess the meaning of the sentence. If nobody guesses correctly, the child must tell everyone the answer.

● Discuss briefly what the child could have done to make the meaning clearer, then invite another child to have a go.

Differentiation
Provide younger or less able children with simple actions such as *Can I fly your kite?*. Encourage the children to think of ways in which they can show what they want, for example, pretending to fly kite and looking up in the sky. Older or more able children could make up their own sentences or situations. Look at ways of explaining how to do something, such as asking for help in an emergency.

AGE RANGE 7–11

LEARNING OBJECTIVE
To understand why different rules are needed in different situations and how to take part in making and changing rules.

CURRICULUM LINKS
KS2: 2b.
QCA Citizenship: Unit 1 – Taking part; Unit 4 – People who help us; Unit 8 – How do rules and laws affect me?

Party rules

What you need
A safe, open space; pens; the 'Party rules' photocopiable sheet on page 96 (one card per child).

What to do
● Cut out the individual cards on the photocopiable sheet.
● With groups of no more than 12, sit the children in a semicircle and give a card to each child. Work together to make up an appropriate rule for each guest, using the chef's card as an example.
● Ask a child to read out their character and rule. For example: *A chef. Rule: Wash hands before you cook.* Ask the children why this rule is important for a chef (to stop the spread of germs).
● Explain that the children are all invited to a party as the character on their card. They must act in character at the party, for example, a dentist would ask to look at the other guests' teeth.
● Start at one end of the semicircle and ask the first child to stand in front of the group. Explain that he or she is the host character of the party and has to pretend to get things ready.
● The next child in the semicircle stands up and calls out *Knock, knock,* and the host character asks *Who is it?.* The child calls out their guest name. For example, *I'm a chef.* The host opens the door and says *The rule of the party is….* At this point the host character says their rule and both children have to follow it.
● Then the next child comes up and says *Knock, knock.* The last child who came in goes to the door and asks for the new guest's name. They then say their rule, and all three children follow the rule.
● The game continues in the same way until the last child in the semicircle joins the party. The last child calls out their rule at the end.
● Each time a rule is mentioned, everyone at the party has to follow it.

Differentiation
Give younger or less able children a scenario, such as school. Sit the children in a circle, and encourage a child to act out a rule in the middle of the circle. Other children should come into the middle of circle to act out other example of school rules. Older and more able children could make up their own roles and rules.

10–Minute Games

BRIGHT IDEAS

Faceless feelings

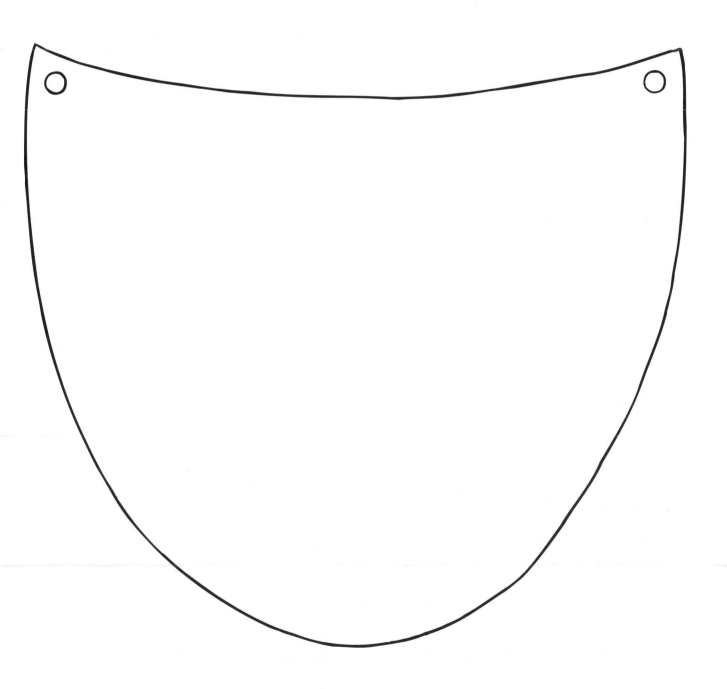

Party rules

Guest: A chef **Rule:** Wash your hands before you cook.	**Guest:** Fire fighter **Rule:**
Guest: Police officer **Rule:**	**Guest:** Lifeguard **Rule:**
Guest: Park keeper **Rule:**	**Guest:** Nurse **Rule:**
Guest: Dentist **Rule:**	**Guest:** Librarian **Rule:**
Guest: Dinner supervisor **Rule:**	**Guest:** Bus driver **Rule:**
Guest: Crossing-patrol person **Rule:**	**Guest:** Magician **Rule:**